"If you're ready to move beyond burnout and build a truly resilient team, CLICKING is your roadmap. Rudnik's five pillars offer a fresh and deeply insightful framework for creating a culture where teams solve problems collaboratively and achieve more, giving leaders the space to finally lead strategically."

—Dr. GLEB TSIPURSKY, Best-Selling Author of *Never Go With Your Gut: How Pioneering Leaders Make the Best Decisions and Avoid Business Disasters*

"In the evolving landscape of corporate business environments, there exists a wild west approach to leadership with little consistency even within a single large company. The result is a lack of engagement from employees and a lack of productivity by companies. CLICKING is the answer. With a powerful 5-part framework, this book clearly demonstrates how companies can increase purpose, communication, and decision-making within teams. It is a must read for any leader or HR officer wanting to excel in the corporate world."

—ERIK SEVERSEN, Bestselling Author of *Ordinary to Extraordinary*

"CLICKING is a masterclass in building real connections and real results, packed with practical exercises, templates, and real-world stories."

—RAYA BELINSKY, President of ICF Israel, executive and team coach.

"As a fellow author focused on modern leadership, I was immediately struck by the clarity and practicality of Daria Rudnik's framework. CLICKING delivers a high-impact, accessible strategy for building teams that operate with purpose, alignment, and self-sufficiency. It's the kind of playbook leaders need to prevent dysfunction from stalling trust, focus, or results."

—TOM MAWHINNEY, Bestselling Author of The Contemporary Leader

CLICKING

CLICKING

A Team Building Strategy for Overloaded
Leaders Who Want Stronger Team Trust, Better
Results, and More Time

DARIA RUDNIK

THIN LEAF PRESS

Publication Data
Name: Rudnik, Daria, Author
Title: CLICKING: A Team Building Strategy for Overloaded Leaders Who Want Stronger Team Trust, Better Results, and More Time

ISBN: 978-1-968318-04-8 (Paperback) | 978-1-968318-05-5 (Hardcover) 978-1-968318-03-1 (eBook)

Business, Money, Management, Leadership
Editor: Dhanliza Cellona
Book Cover Design: 100 Covers
Schemes Design: Sasha Faradzheva
Interior Formatting: Dindo B. Sanguenza.
Thin Leaf Press

THIN
LEAF

TABLE OF CONTENTS

Introduction 1

Part 1: Clear Purpose 5

Chapter 1: Is This Even a Team?
How to Stop Pretending and Start Building One 7
Chapter 2: "Why Are We Here?"
Crafting a Clear Team Purpose... 21
Chapter 3: The Team Constitution:
Your Rules of Engagement.. 39

Part 2: Linking Connections 55

Chapter 4: Strong Teams Are Built Peer-to-Peer,
Not Top-Down 57
Chapter 5: Think Like a Network, Not a Hierarchy 71
Chapter 6: No Team Is an Island: Build Your Ecosystem 85

Part 3: Integrated Work 97

Chapter 7: Stop the Guessing: Nail Roles, Expectations,
and Ownership... 99
Chapter 8: Design Meetings That Drive Progress 113
Chapter 9: Mastering Remote and Hybrid Collaboration........... 129

Part 4: Collaborative Decisions 137

Chapter 10: Brave Decisions, Bold Teams................................... 139
Chapter 11: Who Decides What—and
How to Make It Work... 149
Chapter 12: From Firefighting to Focus: How Top Teams
Prioritize 163

Part 5: Knowledge Sharing 175

    Chapter 13: Ask Better Questions, Get Real Feedback 177
    Chapter 14: Pay Off Your Conflict Debt 189
    Chapter 15: Reflect, Reset, Repeat: Making Growth a Team
    Habit 203

Epilogue: One Step at a Time 215

Index 223

INTRODUCTION

It had been an exhausting week—a transatlantic journey to Peru, followed by a ride on a small, shaky plane to Nicaragua. Now, I was facing the long haul back to Europe. We were setting up new offices all around the globe, and my role was to align our people and processes with headquarters. Now, I had one clear mission: to build the same vibrant culture in every location in the world.

In that moment, waiting for wheels up, I realized I was at an inflection point in my career. The challenge ahead of me was profound—leading a major cultural shift for a fast-growing telecom startup that spanned multiple countries. It was the kind of challenge I had always wanted. I had worked for this opportunity. Yet as I stared out the plane window into the darkness, I couldn't shake the nagging feeling that I wasn't ready. I was exhausted after visiting just three offices. There were dozens left to go. I thought to myself, *It shouldn't be this hard. There's got to be a better way.*

I was running on empty, constantly firefighting, stretched thin by competing priorities and struggling to stay alert to every emerging issue. This left little time for the important, strategic work of building relationships with stakeholders and creating a vibrant culture. Forget planning for the future or empowering my teams to thrive and perform, let alone taking care of my own well-being. I was barely holding it together.

After a lifetime building up to this opportunity, now that I had the job of my dreams, I wasn't enjoying myself. I didn't want to micromanage or solve every problem myself anymore. I couldn't succeed like this, and neither could the company. I had to somehow create a system where teams worked independently, in alignment with the vision of leadership, and yet could confront challenges and solve problems on their own. But how? That question started a 15-year journey to find an answer and a methodology that would allow me to do the job I was hired to do, rather than getting into the scrum with every team member on a daily basis, and exhausting my inner resources.

The world of work has evolved dramatically over the last decade, and certainly as a result of the pandemic, but one thing hasn't changed: Leaders are more overloaded than ever. A recent Microsoft report[1] found that 53% of managers are burned out. Another study by Deloitte[2] found that 68% of leaders identified increased work volume compared to pre-pandemic levels as their top source of stress. These numbers highlight a fundamental problem: The traditional model of leadership—where leaders shoulder the bulk of responsibility and problem-solving—is no longer sustainable. Leaders are burning out. We need a better way to create and maintain interconnected, resilient teams capable of solving problems on their own.

Since that day, as a Chief People Officer and executive coach, I've worked with countless teams in companies at all stages of growth from startups to Fortune 500 giants. Along the way, I developed a framework which I call CLICK, which is my revolutionary method for transforming teams into high-performing, self-sufficient units. This isn't just a collection of best practices—it's a proven strategy, tested across industries, cultures, and team sizes. Over the years, I've worked with leaders facing all kinds of challenges including:

- Overwhelmed managers stuck in reactive, firefighting modes of leadership
- Dysfunctional dynamics caused by poor communication or mistrust

---

[1] Hybrid Work Is Just Work. Are We Doing It Wrong? https://www.microsoft.com/en-us/worklab/work-trend-index/hybrid-work-is-just-work

[2] Well-being and resilience in senior leaders https://www.deloitte.com/content/dam/assets-zone3/ca/en/docs/services/consulting/2024/ca-senior-leader-well-being-resilience-report-2021-en-aoda.pdf?t

- Teams struggling with misalignment and unclear goals
- Teams set up for failure from the start

The CLICK framework addresses all of these elements and more. Whether you're dealing with a disengaged group or looking to elevate an already functional team, CLICK gives you a clear and actionable path forward. The CLICK framework is built around five key pillars:

Clear Purpose: At the heart of every high-performing team is a shared, compelling purpose. It's not just about setting goals; it's about ensuring every team member understands why their work matters.

Linking Connections: Building strong, trusting relationships both within the team and with key stakeholders.

Integrated Work: Establishing clear norms and processes so teams can operate independently.

Collaborative Decisions: Establishing clear decision-making frameworks ensures teams can act decisively and cohesively.

Knowledge Sharing: Creating an environment where knowledge flows freely and feedback is embraced leads to innovation and growth.

Most leadership training focuses on the relationship between leaders and individual team members. While that's important, it's only part of the equation. The real power of leadership lies in building cohesive, self-sufficient teams that can function on their own, with minimal management from the top. When you shift your focus to the team as a whole and learn how to manage team dynamics, you can break free from the cycle of overwork, micro-management, exhausted leadership, and underperforming teams. You'll no longer feel like the sole problem solver or the bottleneck. Instead, you'll have a team that's capable, interdependent, aligned, and self-directing.

This book is for leaders like you—leaders who are ready to move beyond survival mode and build something truly impactful. It's not about perfection; it's about progress. By the end of this book, you'll have the tools and confidence to guide your team toward high performance, one step at a time.

Now, let's get started.

PART 1

CLEAR PURPOSE

"Life is never made unbearable by circumstances, but only by lack of meaning and purpose."

—Viktor Frankl (1905–1997), Austrian neurologist, psychiatrist, and Holocaust survivor

We've all heard a lot about the importance of organizational purpose— the importance of knowing the "why" behind what a company does, why that company exists in the first place. You may have seen your company's mission and vision statements, articulating this "why." They're often on the company's website or explained at introductory events. These statements are usually crafted to inspire and motivate us. But here's the reality: Organizations may have a clear and articulated purpose, but their teams usually don't. And this gap matters a lot.

Let me ask you this: Does your team know *why* it exists? Beyond just what it does every day, does your team know the bigger—and more profound reason—why it matters to the organization and its stakeholders? If you're hesitating, you're not alone. Many teams struggle with this very same question.

A clear team purpose makes work meaningful, and meaningful work is the key to high-performing teams. Without this understanding of the team *why*, it can often feel like we are stumbling around toward nowhere for no apparent reason. Even the most talented members can feel disconnected and lose their sense of direction. They struggle with motivation. They fail to see how their work fits into the bigger picture. And unfocused action is rarely efficient—or inspired. A team with a clear purpose, on the other hand, is a cohesive and strong, high-performing unit.

In this section, we'll explore why a team-specific purpose is the secret sauce that transforms disengaged teams into energized, self-reliant and efficient cells. I'll show you how to define your team's purpose and explain how it differs from the broader organizational vision. And then together, we'll walk through the process of creating a clear, actionable, and inspiring team purpose statement. By the end of this section, you'll grasp the importance of team purpose and have the tools to express it. This will reinvigorate your team and align its efforts with your organization's mission.

Ready? Let's start crafting your team purpose.

CHAPTER 1

IS THIS EVEN A TEAM? HOW TO STOP PRETENDING AND START BUILDING ONE

I've heard people refer to a group of individuals who happen to share a manager as a "team." But let's be real—that's not a team. Most people loosely grouped without a unified mission or connective tissue will barely interact with each other. They will be laser-focused on their individual contributions and meeting their personal performance goals for the sake of their bonuses. These folks generally work in silos, with no sense of collective accountability or common purpose. It takes a lot more than just proximity to one another in a cubicle—and a common manager to make a team.

In today's workplace, we're guilty of throwing around the word "team" far too casually. It means that many leaders fall prey to the dangerous illusion that they have true teamwork, alignment, and collaborative potential working under them; when in reality, they don't at all. This illusion can be costly. It blinds leaders to the gaps in their workforce dynamics and prevents them from taking the deliberate steps needed to foster legitimate collaboration and high performance.

Here's the hard truth: You can't fix what you don't understand or appreciate. When organizations mistakenly believe they already have effective teamwork, there's no incentive to continue to invest. Why tinker with what isn't broken? Leaders boast about these teams to me all the time. They boast about their strong teams in meetings. Their projected results are based on these misunderstandings. Projections are made that a crack team might be able to deliver, but that the actual team cannot hope to produce. When teams aren't aligned, the impact is obvious: Efforts are duplicated, communication breaks down, valuable opportunities slip through the cracks, and promises based on fantasy projections fail to be kept.

So how does a working group become a high-performing team? The journey unfolds in stages, each with its own challenges and opportunities.

Stage 1: Finding Your Footing

Every team starts somewhere. When a new team is formed, it typically begins as a working group. At this stage, people operate independently, focused on their own tasks, with little collaboration or shared accountability. And let's be honest —this is more of a collection of individuals than a true team. But that's okay. Teams don't magically emerge overnight. They require deliberate effort, consistent actions, and time to grow into something greater.

In the beginning, teams often go through what can feel like a messy adjustment period. There's friction, a bit of awkwardness, and maybe even some conflict.[3] This phase is critical. Why? Because it's where norms begin to take shape—both formal and informal. This is when team culture starts to develop.

During this stage, team members are learning to navigate each other's work styles. They might start to recognize the value of collaboration, but they're not quite there yet. Trust is still tentative, and while there may be alignment on some goals, the group hasn't yet unlocked its full potential.

---

[3]   To learn more about stages in group development read Tuckman, Bruce W (1965). "Developmental sequence in small groups". Psychological Bulletin.

Sound familiar? If you've ever been part of a team in this stage, you know how hard it can be to push through the tension.

Stage 2: **Moving Toward Cohesion**

With time and effort, something remarkable begins to happen. The group starts to find its rhythm. Members align their efforts around shared goals, trust begins to grow, and the team becomes more cohesive. This is when things start to click. Suddenly, there's a focus on collective performance, and individuals start to take accountability not just for their own contributions but for the success of the team as a whole.

At this stage, you'll see trust and collaboration deepen. Meetings feel more productive, decision-making becomes more streamlined, and the team operates with greater efficiency. It's what most people think of when they imagine a functional team. But here's the thing: Even a cohesive, effective team hasn't yet hit its peak.

Stage 3: **Reaching Synergy**

True synergy is the ultimate goal—a stage where the team operates as something greater than the sum of its individual parts. This is where high performance and team autonomy truly take off. At this level, the team functions as a unified entity, soaring on the wings of shared purpose and mutual support.

What does synergy look like in action? It's when collaboration feels effortless, trust is unshakable, and leadership is shared across the group. Team members anticipate each other's needs, adapt quickly to challenges, and focus on results that exceed expectations. They don't just perform well— they innovate, problem-solve creatively, and deliver exceptional outcomes.

Teams operating at this level:

- **Work toward shared goals** with a clear sense of collective purpose.

- **Engage in collaborative decision-making,** bringing diverse perspectives to the table.

- **Consider and include stakeholder input,** aligning their work with broader organizational objectives.

Teams that are clicking go beyond high performance; they are not only high-performing but also *self-sufficient*. A self-sufficient team, a real CLICK team, excels in stable conditions but also has the agility and resilience to adapt quickly to changing circumstances and make quick decisions on their own. Such teams take ownership of their success, make decisions independently, and pivot when needed without waiting for top-down direction.

CLICK teams are extremely rare, but when they occur, they are capable of driving lasting impact, fostering innovation, and self-generating a culture where every member feels empowered to contribute their best. They meet goals and redefine what's possible, ensuring that the organization thrives in both predictable and unpredictable environments.

So first of all, if we understand now that the majority of functional units and organizational groups are not teams, how do we define a team? How do we know if we are leading a team or just a work group?

To be considered a team, a group of people must meet certain essential criteria:

The CLICK Team Criteria Checklist

- **A long-term shared purpose:** Each member must be committed to a common purpose—something bigger than themselves. It's not just about short-term tasks or individual performance metrics. True teams have a shared mission that drives them forward, one in which they're all equally invested.

- **Interdependence:** Achieving the team's goals doesn't happen through individual efforts alone. It requires interdependence— where team members not only work together but also rely on each other's strengths, skills, and knowledge. Interdependence means that success is built on mutual trust, not just cooperation. The team must function as a cohesive unit, with each member contributing in a way that directly impacts the team's ability to move forward. It's about creating value together, not just aggregating individual results.

- **A clearly defined team structure:** It should be clear who is on the team and who isn't. This clarity about roles and team composition is critical for accountability and cohesion. You can't have a high-performing team if people don't know where they fit in or what their responsibilities are. These are the non-negotiables. Anything less and you're just a group of people working in close proximity, not a team.

To illustrate, let's take a closer look at two leadership teams—one that struggled and eventually failed, and another that struggled but found a way to rebuild itself and to click into place in the end.

Chaos at the Top

The leadership team at a growing cloud computing company was anything but cohesive. Twenty-five individuals reported directly to the CEO, Sam. Some of the folks were part of the C-Suite, while others held senior roles without the same title. Some attended weekly leadership meetings, while others were excluded. Even within the C-Suite, influence varied—some executives were key decision-makers with the CEO's ear, while others were left out of major conversations. Despite calling this group a "team," it failed to meet the basic CLICK Team Criteria for these reasons:

1. **No Structure**

No one could explain how people became part of this so-called team or what united them. Without a clear structure, there was no defined way to determine membership, roles, or responsibilities. This violated the foundational principle of a well-defined team structure.

2. **No Interdependence**

These individuals didn't rely on one another to succeed. Their only connection was through Sam, who made all the decisions about group assignments and responsibilities. Without interdependence, collaboration was nonexistent, and members operated in silos.

3. **No Shared Purpose**

While they were all working toward broader organizational goals, there was no team-specific purpose. For any leadership team, organizational goals aren't enough. A team needs to understand how it—as a unique entity—contributes to those goals. Even C-Suite teams need their own purpose that aligns with but isn't identical to the organization's mission.

This lack of structure, interdependence, and clear purpose eventually led to the team's downfall. Over time, the cracks widened. New C-Suite members rarely lasted more than two years. During the pandemic, with fewer in-person interactions, communication gaps grew even wider. Sam felt increasingly out of control and resorted to micromanaging, filling his days with back-to-back meetings to resolve conflicts and assign tasks. Sam was exhausted and started losing sight of the bigger picture.

Without clarity or alignment, the leadership team became focused on self-preservation—avoiding blame for missed goals and poor processes. Within a few years, the chaos culminated in the company being absorbed by its parent organization, and most of the leadership team—including Sam—were let go.

Rebuilding Trust

Now, let's look at a contrasting example: a B2G (Business to Government) startup selling complex software solutions to governments in emerging markets. When the founder decided to step back, he hired a promising young sales executive, Jim, to take over as CEO. Jim had a proven track record of selling complex solutions, making him seem like the perfect fit. But there was a major issue: a cultural divide between Jim and the original team assembled by the founder.

While this team had a clear structure, they lacked two critical elements: **shared purpose** and **interdependence**.

- Jim believed he could create the strategy on his own, without input from the team.
- The team, loyal to the founder (now a board member), didn't trust Jim and thought they could bypass him to make decisions directly with the founder.

The situation spiraled into dysfunction. Jim fired one of the executives and brought in his own people, but this only deepened the divide. Now it wasn't just "Jim vs. the old team"—it was "Jim and his people vs. the old team," with added tension from the founder and board. Despite Jim's tireless efforts, the company had no unified strategy, no new sales, and no progress. When I joined to help mediate the situation, it was clear that something had to give. The founder trusted Jim's potential, but the team dynamics were toxic. Everyone recognized the need for a reset, and that's where we started.

The first step was to address **purpose**. The big WHY? What was the purpose of the organization? And more importantly, what was the purpose of the executive team? These were the conversations we had to navigate carefully. At first, I facilitated separate discussions—one with the old team and one with Jim—to gather their thoughts and ideas. I then acted as a bridge, sharing perspectives back and forth. Over time, they began to see common ground and were ready to come together for a full discussion.

Through these conversations, we identified a shared purpose. While the organization's broader mission was to sell complex solutions to governments and improve citizens' access to services, the executive team defined its immediate purpose as *developing the best sales strategy to achieve that larger goal*. This wasn't a long-term purpose, but for the startup's current stage, it was exactly what they needed to understand in order to move forward.

Once we had identified the shared team purpose, it was time to define roles and responsibilities—not based on titles but on each person's unique skills. This shift was critical. By focusing on capabilities rather than hierarchy, the team began to function more interdependently. They recognized that success required collaboration, mutual reliance, and trust.

Within weeks, they created a sales strategy that was approved by the board and began implementing it. What had once been a swamp of conflicts and mistrust transformed into a team aligned around a clear goal. Open communication, shared accountability, and trust replaced the old patterns of division and blame.

These two stories demonstrate the power—and necessity—of structure, interdependence, and shared purpose. Without them, even the most talented teams will flounder, as Sam's leadership team did. But with intentional effort, even a fractured team like Jim's can rebuild itself into a cohesive, high-performing unit.

Critical Questions for Team Leaders

If you're leading a team that feels stuck or divided, ask yourself:

- Does my team have a clear structure?
- Are we truly interdependent, or are we operating in silos?
- Do we have a shared purpose that goes beyond the organization's goals?

The answers to these questions can reveal the next steps you need to take. Building a high-performing team isn't easy, but as Jim's story shows, it's absolutely possible—and the results are worth it.

You might be asking yourself right now: *Is my team a real team or not?* It's an important question, and I have just the tool to help you answer it. The **Team Maturity Questionnaire** below is designed to help you reflect on the current state of your team and determine where it falls on the spectrum of maturity—whether it's a working group, a team, or a high-performing, self-sufficient team.

It's not a traditional assessment tool; instead, it's meant to be an opportunity for reflection for team leaders. By thoughtfully answering the questions, leaders will gain clarity on whether their team operates more like a working group, a standard team, or a high-performing, self-sufficient team. The questions are crafted to help you think about what steps you can take to elevate your team's maturity.

Team Maturity Questionnaire

As a leader, it's crucial to regularly assess your team's effectiveness. This questionnaire will help you and your team understand where you are currently at in team maturity and how you can get closer to becoming a self-sufficient team, unlocking full potential and achieving greater results.

First, answer the questions from your perspective as the leader and calculate your score to establish a baseline understanding. Then, share this questionnaire with your team members.

Once you've collected all the results, you can discuss them with your team and agree on the actions you want to take to move your team toward becoming self-sufficient. Use these results as a starting point for a conversation about where you and your team want to improve.

Rate each statement from 1–5 (1 = Strongly Disagree, 5 = Strongly Agree):

1 = Strongly Disagree: "I don't agree at all with this statement."

3 = Neutral: "I see some strengths but also room for improvement."

5 = Strongly Agree: "This is absolutely true for our team."

Purpose and Goals

This section helps understand if everyone is on the same page regarding the "why" and "what" behind the team's work.

1. I feel confident in explaining our team's shared purpose to others.

2. Our team has clear, collective goals that require input and effort from every team member.

3. My individual goals are aligned with and support the team's overall objectives.

Collaboration and Trust

This section highlights the dynamics between team members and how comfortable they are in sharing and receiving feedback.

1. We regularly ask for and listen to each other's input and ideas.

2. We openly share information, resources, and expertise to help each other succeed.

3. When mistakes or failures occur, we discuss them constructively to learn and improve.

Decision-Making and Autonomy

This section explores the team's ability to make independent decisions and manage conflict.

1. Our team can make most decisions independently, without needing approval from outside the team.

2. I feel comfortable respectfully challenging my teammates' ideas, and I value when my own ideas are challenged.

3. We handle disagreements and conflicts in a way that helps us find better solutions.

Accountability and Results

This section assesses how committed each member is to achieve both individual and collective goals.

1. Everyone on the team follows through on their commitments to one another.

2. We regularly recognize and celebrate both individual and team successes in a way that boosts morale.

3. As a team, we consistently deliver results that exceed expectations.

Scoring and Action Plan:

Once you've answered all the questions, calculate your score by adding up the responses for all 12 questions. This will help you determine where your team stands in terms of maturity and effectiveness.

Total Score:

12-30: Working Group

- **What This Means**: Your team may still be in the early stages of development. You may have some collaboration, but there may be a lack of shared goals, trust, and accountability.
- **Action Steps**: Focus on building trust, setting clear goals, and improving communication. Consider regular check-ins to align your team's direction and foster collaboration.

31-48: Team

- **What This Means**: Your team is progressing but may still need improvement in areas like autonomy and deep collaboration. You might still rely on external direction at times.
- **Action Steps**: Encourage more self-direction and accountability within the team. Work on giving your team more autonomy in decision-making and foster stronger, more open communication.

49-60: Self-Sufficient Team

- **What This Means**: Your team is highly collaborative, self-sufficient, and consistently exceeds expectations. Your team is strong in both accountability and performance.

- **Action Steps**: Continue strengthening your team's communication and problem-solving abilities. Celebrate successes and reflect on ways to maintain and even further improve team dynamics.

No matter your score, remember this is only the starting point. If your team's score is low, see it as an opportunity to grow. Think of what's possible when your team starts to click—and becomes a team that not only boosts organizational performance but also creates a more fulfilling work culture where members feel engaged and motivated. Together, you'll deliver exceptional results for your stakeholders while also fostering a sense of pride and fulfillment that extends beyond work to your families and communities.

If your score is high, congratulations! You've done an incredible job building a real team. But even high-performing teams face challenges as they evolve or navigate changing environments. Use what you have learned to help your team tackle obstacles and continue operating at their best.

The Power of Purpose

A question I hear a lot is: *What if my unit isn't designed to function as a team?* Maybe you work together because you have similar roles, but the nature of your work doesn't require a shared purpose or interdependence. That's a valid concern, but let me share a story that might change your perspective.

I was called in to assess the teams at a telecom contact center. Their job was to answer incoming client calls and help solve simple technical issues. At first glance, you might assume they only met one of the three team criteria: a clear structure. There didn't seem to be a need for shared purpose or interdependence with a mission like this. But this contact center was different—they didn't want to work in silos, and they refused to see their role as limited to answering calls. They wanted more meaning in their work, and they found it.

They identified their team purpose as: *making clients' lives easier.* This meant that even if a client called about an issue unrelated to their company's technology, they would still go the extra mile to help. Their interdependence came from mutual learning and maintaining a shared knowledge database. By documenting every problem they solved, they made it easier for others to address similar issues in the future.

The results were remarkable. When the company hit hard times and leadership aimed to cut costs, the contact center became a target. The idea was simple: Shorten call times to save money. However, the CEO, aware of the contact center's mission, approached them differently. He said, "I know your mission is to make our clients' lives easier. And I know that sometimes solving problems the right way takes time. But we're in a difficult period and need to save costs. I'm not imposing strict KPIs for call times, but I ask you to be mindful of the time and help us aim for an average of two minutes per call."

The team could have ignored this request—they weren't being forced to change, and their mission remained intact. But they saw the CEO and the organization as their clients, too, and they wanted to make life easier for them as well. Within a month, they reduced the average call time from 3.5 minutes to just under 2 minutes, all while maintaining their high satisfaction ratings and saving the company millions of dollars.

Even in roles that may not seem like traditional teams, finding a shared purpose and fostering interdependence can spark incredible results. Whether your team is a contact center, a project group, or an executive leadership team, the principles remain the same: Structure, purpose, and interdependence are the building blocks of maturity and high performance.

The journey to building a self-sufficient team starts with honest reflection and self-awareness. It isn't always easy to take a long look at yourself in the mirror. The Team Maturity Questionnaire is the perfect place to begin. Use it as a tool to understand where you are and where you want to go. Every step forward brings your team closer to becoming a cohesive, resilient unit that delivers exceptional results and creates a lasting impact.

CHAPTER 2

"WHY ARE WE HERE?" CRAFTING A CLEAR TEAM PURPOSE

As we have seen, a CLICK team is about more than just showing up and checking tasks off a list. It's about understanding why you do what you do. This is where a clear team purpose comes in. A compelling purpose guides the team through uncertainty, but also created alignment, keeping everyone moving in the same direction.

If you want more clarity on the definitions, here are the definitions of the three most commonly used terms:

- **Vision** represents an inspiring future state or achievement that an organization aspires to achieve.
- **Mission** defines what the organization is currently doing and its path to achieving the vision.
- **Purpose** explains why the organization exists.

The other question you might ask is "how does your team's purpose relates to the purpose of your organization?"

I once sat down with Lara, the chief finance officer of a health tech company, who confided in me a challenge that may sound familiar. "I'm struggling to create a sense of purpose within my team," she admitted.

Sure, the company had a noble mission—to help people live healthier lives—but her finance team felt like any other finance team at any other company. "How can I ignite a sense of purpose that unites us, strengthens our communication, and inspires my team to show up every day, whether they're in the office or working on a spreadsheet remotely?" she asked.

She raised an important point. After all, how many of us have felt a disconnect between our roles and the greater mission? When I asked her how she defined the purpose of her finance team, she recalled a team vision that was created five years ago, long before she joined. "Maybe it's time we revisited it together," she mused.

Organizational Alignment

A clear and overarching team purpose statement drives cohesion and creates alignment. When employees understand their collective mission, they become more motivated and focused. This leads to measurable results that would be hard to achieve otherwise. Simply put, when everyone knows where they're going, they're more likely to get there—and get there faster.

However, having an organizational purpose is not enough. Every team needs a distinct team purpose that connects to the organizational purpose but goes even further. It should clarify why the team itself was created, why these specific individuals were brought together, and what they can aspire to achieve.

A clear team purpose enables the development of a team vision that guides the team's efforts in a common direction despite the differences among team members. This shared sense of purpose reduces ambiguity and conflict, ensuring everyone understands not only the "what" but also the "why" behind their tasks.

Let's face it: When you're on a team and you don't know what you're working toward, it's easy to get lost in the weeds—distracted by the day-to-day demands without a sense of the bigger picture. But with a strong, well-communicated vision, you're more likely to stay focused and resilient when challenges arise. A clearly defined team purpose keeps members focused on the task at hand, helps them coordinate their diverse skills, and enables individuals to learn faster.

In addition, a clear purpose statement reduces internal conflict and speeds decision-making. Studies[4] have found that teams with ambiguous goals often devolved into debate and wasted time as members pulled in different directions. On the other hand, when a team's mission is clear, there's less room for confusion and conflict. Less time wasted on reaching accord. An unclear team vision fosters conflict and mistrust within a team about expectations and outcomes, leading to constant adjustments, debates, and time-consuming processes.

I outlined the definitions of Vision, Mission, and Purpose earlier, and as I mentioned, these terms are often used interchangeably to explain the "why" behind a team and clarify the reason it was created. Once the purpose is clear, the next step is to define goals and tasks. In this book, we'll break these down into three levels:

- **Strategic goals** – Long-term objectives that are essential for the team to fulfill its purpose.

- **Tactical goals** – Short-term priorities, typically spanning six to twelve months, that support the achievement of strategic goals.

- **Tasks** – Day-to-day operational activities that ensure the team makes progress toward its goals.

So how can you foster this sense of purpose in your own team, especially if you're leading remotely? You can start by implementing tools and activities designed to build that common foundation—a clear team vision that unites and inspires.

---

[4]   Lynn, Gary & Kalay, Faruk. (2015). The Effect of Vision and Role Clarity on Team Performance. Pressacademia. 4. 473-473. 10.17261/ Pressacademia.2015313067.

The Team Purpose Statement Template

The Team Purpose Statement template is a practical tool designed to help teams articulate their shared purpose in a clear, concise, and motivating way. It's essentially a mission statement that answers the fundamental question: Why does this team exist? A Team Purpose Statement is a declaration that expresses the team's core reason for existing and effectively communicates its value to the organization and its impact on stakeholders. It's the "why" behind everything the team does. A strong purpose statement is:

- **Clear and concise:** It should be easy to understand and communicate.
- **Inspiring**: It should energize the team by connecting their work to something bigger and more meaningful.
- **Actionable**: It should guide the team's activities and inform day-to-day decisions.

A compelling team purpose brings clarity, meaning, and motivation to the forefront. Here are examples that meet these criteria:

Clear and Concise

- *Example*: "Our purpose is to create a customer onboarding process that makes new users feel confident and empowered from day one."
- **Why it works**: This purpose is straightforward and specific, giving the team a clear sense of what they're here to do and how they add value to the organization.

Inspiring

- *Example*: "Our purpose is to empower small businesses by providing financial tools that simplify their lives and help them achieve their dreams."

- **Why it works**: This purpose ties the team's efforts to a larger, emotionally meaningful mission. It's not just about tasks—it's about making a real impact.

Actionable

- *Example*: "Our purpose is to minimize system downtime to under 0.01%, ensuring uninterrupted service and building customer trust every day."
- **Why it works**: This purpose is tied directly to specific, measurable actions, giving the team clear guidance for their daily priorities and decisions.

When all three qualities are present, the purpose not only unites the team but also fuels their drive to excel. For instance:

- *Example*: "Our purpose is to deliver innovative solutions that empower educators to connect with students and inspire better learning outcomes."
- **Why it works**: This purpose is clear (focused on educators and students), inspiring (helping to improve education), and actionable (providing innovative solutions that deliver measurable results).

Reasons Why Purpose Statements Can Miss Their Mark

Too Vague or Generic

- *Example*: "Our purpose is to support the company's goals."
- **Why it fails**: It's so broad and generic that it provides no meaningful guidance or direction for the team.

Not Inspiring

- *Example*: "Our purpose is to complete all assigned tasks on time."

- **Why it fails**: While being timely is important, this purpose lacks emotional resonance or a connection to something bigger. It feels routine and uninspiring.

Not Actionable

- *Example*: "Our purpose is to change the world through innovative solutions."
- **Why it fails**: While it sounds lofty, it's too abstract to guide day-to-day decisions or help team members understand how their work contributes to the goal.

When a purpose misses the mark, it leaves teams working in silos or feeling unsure of their contributions. Without a clear and meaningful "why," alignment and motivation suffer.

The Team Purpose Statement Template

The Team Purpose Statement Template provides a structured approach to creating a purpose statement that resonates with the entire team. Here's a breakdown of how to use it:

1. Identify key stakeholders and impact

Who does the team serve? (e.g., customers, internal departments, the community)

What impact does the team want to have? (e.g., deliver better products, improve efficiency, increase customer satisfaction)

Identifying key stakeholders helps the team focus on who they work for and why their work is important. For example, "Our team serves internal customers by providing innovative, easy-to-use tools that improve productivity and collaboration."

When a U.S.-based nonprofit I was consulting for sat down to create their team purpose statement, they got right to the heart of their mission by defining their key stakeholders and the impact they wanted to have: *We want to empower older adults to have more autonomy and control over their lives, increase their engagement in the community, and improve the overall quality of life for aging adults.*

As this statement was read, the room fell silent. It was a powerful, almost palpable moment. The words resonated deeply with everyone in the room and struck at the heart of why they were there. It wasn't just a statement—it was a call to action, a shared belief that what they were doing had the potential to change lives. The emotional weight of this purpose was undeniable, and you could see it on their faces. This was more than a mission on paper; it was a clear team purpose statement that had the power to guide their every step, to make every decision more intentional and meaningful.

That's the difference a well-crafted team purpose statement can make—it brings clarity, direction and, most importantly, a sense of purpose that can reignite passion and drive within the team.

2. Define the team's core function

This is simply defining in clear terms, "What does the team do?" (e.g., develop products, manage operations, provide support)

How does the team accomplish its tasks? (e.g., through collaboration, innovation, or customer-centric approaches)

This step helps clarify what the team does at a basic level. For example, "We develop innovative software solutions that enable our users to efficiently achieve their goals."

When one nonprofit I worked with set out to define its core function, it captured the essence of its collaborative approach with a statement that perfectly reflected its mission: *We work with public and private organizations to create, promote, and manage services that meet the diverse needs of older adults in our community.*

This wasn't just a box-ticking exercise in creating a mission statement—it was a clear articulation of how they work and the impact they want to have. By focusing on collaboration with both public and private entities, they acknowledged that the needs of older adults are complex and multifaceted, requiring a unified approach. Their statement emphasized not only the creation of services but also the promotion and management of those services to ensure sustainability and reach.

This kind of clarity in core function is critical. It serves as a compass, a North Star that guides every partnership, every decision, and every initiative. And for this team, it wasn't just about words on a page—it was about building meaningful, lasting relationships to better serve the aging population.

3. Connect to the organization's broader mission

How does the team's work contribute to the organization's overall mission or strategic goals?

This is where you connect the team's purpose to the larger organizational context, ensuring alignment with the company's direction. For example: "By creating innovative solutions, we help the company maintain its market leadership and drive long-term growth."

For one nonprofit, the connection to the broader mission sounded like this: *By improving access to health care and community resources for seniors, our work supports the broader mission of improving health, equity, and healthcare in the county, especially for underserved populations.*

4. Create an Inspirational Team Statement

Using the answers to the previous questions, create a purpose statement that is short, engaging, and easy to remember, that inspires the whole team by highlighting your team's unique value and core goals.

A sample inspiring team purpose statement might look like this:

"Our purpose is to deliver innovative software solutions that enable our customers to work smarter and more efficiently, helping the company achieve its strategic vision of market leadership."

This statement does four important things:

- It defines the impact the team wants to have on its stakeholders.
- It explains what the team does.

- It aligns the team's purpose with the broader goals of the organization.

- It inspires the whole team with the meaning behind its collective action.

For the nonprofit, here was the final statement:

Our purpose is to empower and support seniors in the county by promoting equitable access to essential resources, services, and collaborative partnerships. Through coordinated efforts, we promote the independence, community involvement, and overall well-being of older adults. Aligned with the County's commitment to health equity, we strive to create an age-friendly community where every senior and their support system can thrive with dignity and security.

Implementing the Team Purpose Statement Template

Facilitate a discussion: Gather the team in a collaborative setting. Encourage everyone to share their understanding of the team's current goals and the value they provide. This is critical to gaining buy-in and aligning perspectives.

Use the template: Guide the discussion by using the template to answer key questions about stakeholders, impact, core function, and alignment with the organization's mission.

Craft the purpose statement: Based on the team's input, write a draft of the purpose statement. Keep it concise but inspiring.

Get feedback: Circulate the draft statement to the team and key stakeholders. Make any necessary adjustments to ensure it resonates with everyone.

Communicate and reinforce: Once finalized, communicate the purpose statement widely within the team. Reinforce it regularly in meetings, reviews, and team communications to keep the purpose top of mind.

Joe Takes a Stand

I met Joe, a senior marketing executive at FastGrowingCompany Inc. when I was called in to smooth out the bumps that occur during restructuring. The organization recently went through a series of organizational changes, and Joe had ended up with a newly restructured team. He now led a team that used to be two separate units, and they were struggling to find common ground and work collaboratively. Instead, they were relying heavily on Joe to handle all the communication between these two sub teams. It didn't make things any easier that the team was spread out across different cities, with one team close to where Joe was and the other, newly added part of the team in another location.

The team was split into two distinct units, each with its own history, work style, and expectations. These sub-teams rarely communicated with each other, preferring instead to escalate conflicts directly to Joe. It's a classic case of silos within a team, where collaboration has broken down and a common sense of purpose is clearly missing.

Joe, who was well liked as a person by both sub-teams, found himself in a difficult situation. He was trying to unite the group, but his efforts were being met with apathy at best and resistance at worst. Team members seemed content to let Joe shoulder the burden of problem solving, showing little initiative to address issues themselves. More troubling, each sub-team believed that Joe should take a firmer stance with the other group, effectively asking him to choose sides in their ongoing conflicts.

How can I fix this? Joe kept asking me and himself. He wanted desperately to understand how to turn this group of people into a cohesive team that worked together, supported each other, and more importantly, saw that they were all serving the same purpose—attracting more customers to the company and providing the best cloud solution.

Joe's situation is not unique. In fact, it's common in many organizations where reorganizations, mergers, or rapid growth have brought together people with different skills and approaches. The challenge is not only to manage the day-to-day tasks but also to create a shared vision that can unite these disparate elements into a cohesive, high-performing new team.

After a few months on the job, Joe called his team together for a team meeting where he explained that they were going to work together to define a clear, shared team purpose for their newly formed team. After the first meeting, they were able to come up with a first draft of the team purpose statement. The next day seemed like every other day leading up to the meeting. There were still two very different subgroups, and they were still wary of each other. But something had changed. There were pauses before some of the accusations. There were some words and phrases from yesterday's conversation that everyone seemed to agree on. The process of finding a common language and mutual understanding had begun.

Joe knew that this was only the first small step. But even that step had managed to change the dynamics of the team's work.

When SMART goals are not enough

After you have defined your team's purpose statement, the next step is to make it more actionable and translate the purpose into strategic team goals. A widely taught management practice, emphasized in countless training programs, is the importance of setting SMART goals—which is an amazing tool—but we will add an extra layer to it.

The acronym SMART stands for Specific, Measurable, Achievable[5], Relevant, and Time-bound. These goals were originally designed to bring structure and clarity to goal setting, and in stable environments, they can be incredibly effective. But there's a challenge: In environments of constant change, rigidly focusing on SMART goals can stifle creativity, agility, and motivation. When teams are limited to static goals and objectives, they often shy away from taking risks. Instead of chasing new, potentially transformative opportunities, they settle for what feels safe and achievable.

---

[5] Originally Assignable, first introduced in Doran, G. T. (1981). "There's a S.M.A.R.T. way to write management's goals and objectives". Management Review.

Overly rigid goals can encourage underperformance. If team members feel they must hit their targets exactly, they won't push beyond their comfort zones. SMART goals can unintentionally hinder innovation and limit teams' ability to adapt in a rapidly changing environment.

Maya Makes Her Move

As the new year approached, Maya gathered her leadership team for their annual goal-setting retreat. She was determined to make this year different. In previous years, they had diligently followed the SMART goal framework, setting specific, measurable, achievable, relevant, and time-bound objectives for each department. Yet, despite their best efforts, the company had struggled to adapt to sudden market shifts and emerging opportunities.

"I don't know about you," Maya began, "but I'm starting to think our SMART goals aren't always so smart." She shared a recent conversation with a fellow CEO who had inadvertently created a culture of mediocrity by tying bonuses strictly to goal achievement. "People were setting easy targets just to secure their bonuses. We need a better way."

Like Maya, many leaders believe that SMART goals (Specific, Measurable, Achievable, Relevant, and Time-bound) are the gold standard. And while they do have merits, especially in stable environments, they can fall short in today's fast-paced, ever-changing business landscape. We need something more adaptive and dynamic to meet the demands of real-world teams.

Goal Posts That Can Move

Today's success often depends on your team's ability to pivot, adapt, and innovate as new challenges arise. This is where traditional SMART goals miss the mark—they don't account for the need to evolve as circumstances change. So, what can we do instead?

Here are more adaptive strategies that can help your team not only survive but thrive in a constantly changing environment:

1. **Align goals with organizational purpose**

Teams thrive when they understand how their work contributes to the organization's larger mission. Team members can become unmotivated and disengaged when goals feel mandated from high. Rather than dictating goals from the top down, involve your teams in the goal-setting process. Engage them in discussions of business objectives and organizational purpose, then collaborate to develop measurable, motivating targets.

According to McKinsey's research, 70% of employees[6] define their sense of purpose through work. Connecting team goals to the broader organizational purpose inspires a sense of meaning and dedication to the work. This approach enhances both morale and performance and leads to increased productivity.

2. **Break down silos through collaborative goal setting**

It is important to remember that a team is defined by a shared purpose. When members focus on individual goals, it can fragment teams. You don't want each team member to pursue personal success in isolation. A CLICK team aligns around shared goals whose objectives can only be achieved through collaboration.

So prioritize collective goals instead of encouraging your team to chase separate targets or quotas. Prompt every member to work together to accomplish these goals. This approach builds cohesion and keeps the team aligned. It increases the team's impact beyond what any one person could achieve.

In today's complex work environment, cross-functional collaboration is critical. Setting goals in isolation can prevent teams from recognizing interdependencies and taking advantage of the strengths of other departments. It is vital to encourage teams to identify key stakeholders and partners that are crucial to achieving their objectives.

---

[6] Help your employees find purpose—or watch them leave https:// www.mckinsey.com/capabilities/people-and-organizational-performance/ our-insights/help-your-employees-find-purpose-or-watch-them-leave

3. Deploy Stretch Goals with built-in room for error

While SMART goals emphasize achievability, Stretch Goals push teams to aim higher, encouraging innovation and creativity. The key is to strike a balance between ambition and realism. Stretch goals should be bold enough to inspire your team to think outside the box but not so extreme that they feel impossible or overwhelming. However, one crucial element often overlooked is building intentional room for error.

This margin for error is essential because not everything will go according to plan in complex and unpredictable environments. Your team might need more time, additional resources, or even a complete shift in strategy to adapt to unforeseen circumstances. By allowing for this flexibility, you empower your team to take calculated risks and experiment without the fear of failure hanging over their heads.

For instance, if your team estimates a project will take six weeks, consider extending the timeline by 25%. This extra time provides a buffer for unexpected challenges, shifts in priorities, or external factors beyond your control, all without the looming pressure of missing a hard deadline. Along the way, break down the project into mini-milestones to ensure the team stays on track and can make adjustments as needed.

The goal here is not to lower your standards but to recognize that no plan is flawless. Build in space for your team to pivot, extend deadlines, or reallocate resources as they navigate the inevitable bumps along the way. This helps keep your team from burning out and creates a space where new ideas can flourish.

Stay humble and flexible—accept that there are always factors outside of your control. By giving your team the room to adapt and recalibrate, you ensure they remain focused on the bigger picture rather than getting bogged down by day-to-day hurdles.

4. Distinguish between learning goals and performance goals

When it comes to setting goals, one of the biggest challenges is figuring out what kind of goal your team actually needs. Are you trying to hit a measurable target, or is this about innovation and moving the team forward? That's where **performance goals** and **learning goals** come in. While performance goals focus on achieving specific targets, learning goals center on acquiring new knowledge and skills. They're both important, but they serve very different purposes—and knowing when to use each is one key to setting your team up for success.

Performance goals are the goals we're all familiar with. They're about achieving specific, measurable results. These are the "What do we need to accomplish?" goals, and they're great for providing clarity and keeping the team focused.

For example:

- Increase sales in a region by 10%.
- Launch a new product by the end of the quarter.
- Cut customer complaints by 20%.

Performance goals work best when the task is clear-cut or familiar—when your team knows the territory and has a good idea of how to get there. They give everyone a clear target to aim for, and they're a great way to hold people accountable.

But there's a downside. If performance goals are too rigid, they can actually limit creativity. Teams can end up so focused on "hitting the number" that they shy away from bold ideas or risks. They stick to what they know even if it's not the best long-term approach.

Learning goals, on the other hand, are about growth. They're focused on the process of gaining new skills, testing ideas, or finding solutions—not just checking a box. These goals answer the question: *How do we need to change to succeed?*

For example:

- Experiment with three new sales strategies in an untapped market.
- Learn advanced features of a CRM tool to improve customer engagement.

- Run tests to figure out what really drives customer behavior.

Learning goals are ideal when the path forward isn't clear or when your team needs to adapt to something new. They encourage experimentation, risk-taking, and creativity—things you can't always do when there's pressure to hit a specific number.

Performance and learning goals aren't a binary choice. You need both. In fact, they often go hand in hand. If you want to increase sales in a region by 10%, that might be your performance goal. Along with that, a team might aim to develop and test three innovative growth strategies for that market. Together, they create a balance between innovation and accountability.

Here's why you need both:

- **Performance goals** keep the team focused and deliver measurable results.
- **Learning goals** build new skills, foster creativity, and help the team prepare for bigger challenges.

If you lean too heavily on performance goals, you risk stifling innovation—your team might stick to what feels safe instead of taking risks and learning new things. But conversely, if you only focus on learning goals, you might end up with a lot of great ideas that never turn into action.

5. **Making goal-setting a team habit**

Embedding goal-setting into the daily routine encourages teams to stay focused and aligned. Teams that regularly set and review goals are more likely to achieve their Key Performance Indicators (KPIs) and report higher levels of job satisfaction[7]. This practice boosts morale and creates a culture of accountability and continuous improvement.

---

[7] Pervaiz, Sabeeh & Li, Guohao & Qi, He. (2021). The mechanism of goal-setting participation's impact on employees' proactive behavior, moderated mediation role of power distance. PLOS ONE. 16. e0260625. 10.1371/journal.pone.0260625.

Celebrate small wins to maintain high morale. Recognizing achievements—no matter how minor—can elevate team mood and increase engagement. Sharing successes fosters a supportive environment where team members feel valued and motivated to contribute their best work.

Reflection Questions

- Does your team have a clear understanding of why it exists and how its work impacts the broader organization?

- How can you articulate your team's purpose in a way that inspires action and aligns with the organization's mission?

- What steps can you take to ensure that every team member is aligned with the purpose statement?

For teams to succeed in today's world, they need a good mix of structure and flexibility! The Team Purpose Statement helps teams know their shared mission. A modern approach to goal-setting lets them adapt as conditions change. When teams combine clear purpose with dynamic goals, they can maintain direction while having the freedom to innovate. This approach boosts team performance. It gives members clarity and space to evolve. What matters most is that teams understand what they're doing and why they're doing it and have the tools to adjust their path when needed.

CHAPTER 3

THE TEAM CONSTITUTION: YOUR RULES OF ENGAGEMENT

Now that your team has a clear purpose and a well-articulated team purpose statement, the next step to becoming a CLICK team is to define how you will work together to achieve your stated purpose. To build a truly cohesive CLICK team, you must define how your team will function on a daily basis. This is where your team's values and norms begin to shape behavior.

Every team operates by a set of values—whether they've been explicitly defined or not. These values reflect what's important to your team members and shape how you approach work and interact with one another. Take the time to intentionally discuss and agree on your team's values, ensuring that everyone knows what forces will guide decisions and behavior. While your team's values should align with your organization's overall culture, they should also reflect what's uniquely important to your team and align with individual team members. Values are at the foundation of team interaction, collaboration, and decision-making. Without clearly defined values that have been accepted by all team members, your team will inevitably face conflicts

As a Chief People Officer in a B2G technology startup, I coached two executives who clashed over how our purpose should be accomplished. One of the executives pushed for speed and shorter time-to-market, while the other prioritized the high quality of the product. While both were fully engaged in our organizational purpose, they had a conflict of values as it related to action—speed versus quality. This conflict was only resolved after the executive team came together to identify our shared team values, prioritize them, and establish norms—behaviors through which those values were demonstrated and executed.

Values on their own won't drive action. Team leaders need to walk their talk, establish norms, and bring these values to life. Team norms are the specific, agreed-upon behaviors that translate your values into practice. While norms often begin as unspoken rules that shape how people work together, they work far better when explicitly defined.

How will your team communicate? What's your approach to decision-making? How will you handle disagreements? These are the questions that norms answer. Setting clear expectations early helps avoid misunderstandings and misaligned behaviors later on. It also creates a straightforward framework for respectful and consistent teamwork that reflects your team's core values.

This chapter explores how to define your team's values and translate them into actionable norms. These elements will ensure your team operates with clarity, consistency, and alignment. When team members agree upon shared values and norms, the team now has a bridge between its purpose and how you work to achieve it. Let's dive in and define the engagement rules that will shape how your team can put purpose into motion and click.

Rebuilding the Core

In 2007, I joined a bank to lead their learning and development function. Just two weeks into the job, the bank's license was suspended for three months. It was a seismic event that shook the foundation of the organization. Suddenly, we couldn't serve our customers. There was nothing to do until the situation resolved, yet we had to keep all of our employees engaged and ready to resume operations as soon as we were licensed. We had to improve our operations according to the central bank's guidelines, all while managing the uncertainty that hung over us.

This was the first major crisis I had to deal with as a leader, and let me tell you, it was a transformative experience. Instead of succumbing to panic, we saw opportunity. We used that time to revisit our corporate values and breathe new life into our corporate principles.

We involved nearly every employee in focus groups and communications campaigns during our downtime. We didn't just dictate values from the top down; we worked together to redefine who we were and what we stood for. This collective effort wasn't just about checking a box—it was about reigniting a common purpose that everyone could rally behind even during a time of enormous disruption and confusion.

We used that unified spirit to make things right for the bank and to show the regulator that we were committed to excellence. Remarkably, we retained all of our employees during those tumultuous three months—not a single person left voluntarily. We emerged more connected and united, feeling that these values were not just words on a wall but living, breathing principles that had helped us succeed in a difficult time.

This experience reinforced for me the incredible power of a shared vision put into action. It was a time when we let go of our individual ambitions and focused on what was right for the organization and our clients, with everyone pulling in the same direction. It gives meaning to the daily grind and inspires people to do their best even in the face of adversity.

During this process, we realized that values alone weren't enough to provide the clarity the organization needed. We needed to go deeper—offering not just words to inspire but actionable principles to guide everyday decisions and behaviors. In response, they enhanced our values framework with something far more robust: a corporate constitution.

Creating a Team Constitution

The team constitution we created in that moment wasn't just a list of abstract values; it was a set of clear, guiding principles that outlined both what the company stood for and how employees should approach their work. It provided the clarity teams needed to align their individual goals with the organization's overarching goals. The constitution addressed common pitfalls by explicitly describing behaviors that fostered trust, encouraged collaboration, and allowed room for creativity while keeping everyone moving in the same direction.

Rather than simply stating that employees should be ambitious, the constitution detailed what healthy ambition looked like—balancing hard work with respect for personal time and supporting team success over individual competition. By defining not just values but the principles behind them, the company was able to create a shared understanding of how to achieve success in a way that was consistent with the company's mission and culture.

This shift to a principles-based constitution allowed the company to maintain its agility as it grew. Employees, regardless of department or seniority, had a clear sense of how their work fit into the larger goals of the organization. Teams could operate with a degree of autonomy, but still within clear rules, because the principles they were expected to follow were laid out for them in advance, keeping everyone aligned and accountable to the broader company mission.

In sum, by moving beyond values to clearly articulated principles to an actionable constitution based on norms and values, the company was able to maintain alignment and clarity of purpose across a rapidly growing workforce. This approach ensured that as the company scaled, its teams remained unified, motivated, aligned on core values, and clear on the what and the how of their work.

One of the greatest companies I worked with adopted a principle of doing things "the way it should be." Here's how they explained it: *We all know the world we'd like to live in. It's a world where everyone keeps their promises, work is exciting, and things live up to our expectations. We are just trying to make this world a reality. Doing this isn't easy, but imagining the way things should be in your world is a good place to start.*

Together as a team, a team constitution defines and codifies your team's values, identifies the key principles your team must follow, and provides a guide to decision-making, hiring, recognition, and firing.

Learning from 3M: Values in Action

3M, a global leader in innovation, brings its values to life through actionable principles. They walk their talk, and their entire organization, as well as their customers, know this. The global company has only three core values[8], and they are clearly linked to expected behaviors.

1. **Curiosity**—and they don't just leave it at that. 3M explains their emphasis on curiosity in a way that makes if actionable for their employees: *If you are a naturally curious person and like to ask a lot of questions, you'll be in good company at 3M. In fact, our employees are so curious that we encourage them to devote 15% of their work time to passion projects that wouldn't fall under their normal job description. What we label* **15% Culture** *is actually how the Post-it Note® and other great products were invented!*

This description not only defines the meaning of value of curiosity at 3M—it shows exactly what sort of behavior this is expected to motivate in their workers (asking questions, spending time on passion projects, doing more than the minimum) and explains why it matters (because it leads to great innovation). With this policy, 3M has turned values into principles by moving abstract concepts into the realm of concrete actions that shape the way a team works.

The other two 3M values, **creativity** and **collaboration**, are just as impactful. Creativity fuels their ability to develop innovative solutions, while collaboration ensures that ideas are shared, refined, and brought to life through teamwork. Together, these values enable 3M to create products that make life easier—not just in everyday contexts like office supplies but also in critical industries such as healthcare, electronics, and energy. And it has turned them into a legacy giant in their sector.

---

[8]   What do 3Mers value? https://www.3m.com/3M/en_US/careers-us/stay-connected/insights-for-candidates/full-story/?storyid=9e23eb7e-cceb-4285-86b0-f3a2f28650f9

When values are connected to a clear purpose and translated into everyday actions, they stop being just nice words on paper. They become a practical guide for how your team makes decisions, takes action, and achieves its goals. This kind of alignment doesn't just inspire folks—it leads to real results that benefit both the team and the organization as a whole.

Defining Values: The "How" of Team Behavior

So how do you define the values that truly resonate with your team? Here's a simple, effective strategy that has worked for teams in high-stakes environments, such as the HR transformation unit of a telecommunications company responsible for leading 100,000 employees through a period of significant change. By following these steps, you can ensure that your team's values are not only meaningful but also directly influence their daily actions. And if you're looking for more structured help, you can download an editable template on my website to guide you.

To get started, set aside about two hours for this team meeting. Gather your team members in an environment that encourages open and honest conversation. Begin by clarifying the goal: to define a set of core values that will not only reflect the team's identity but also guide daily behavior. Explain that this is not a one-sided exercise, but a collaborative process designed to foster alignment and a shared sense of purpose.

Begin with a simple icebreaker. Ask each person to take a minute to share their expectations for the session or their initial thoughts about the team's values. A prompt like, "What values do you think are important for our team to thrive?" works well. This warm-up will help everyone start thinking about what truly matters to them and the team.

Exercise: "The Values Card Sort"

Defining your team's values is one of the most important steps you can take to create a strong, shared foundation for how you work together. Let's face it—values aren't just a "nice to have." They shape how decisions are made, how conflicts are resolved, and how your team interacts on a daily basis.

Without clarity on your values, you run the risk of misalignment, where team members interpret what's important in completely different ways.

The Values Card Sort exercise is effective because it actively involves your team. This hands-on activity helps you determine what is most important while ensuring that everyone's voice is included in the process. You'll walk away with a set of values that aren't just inspiring words but an authentic reflection of what your team stands for and how you operate together. Defining what your team stands *for* also involves clarifying the boundaries—the attitudes or behaviors your team stands *against* because they undermine your collective purpose and identity.

Ready to make your team's values real? Let's get started.

Objective

To identify and prioritize the core values that define the team or organization, fostering alignment and commitment.

Setup

1. Materials for In-Person Teams:

- A deck of cards with a variety of values written on them (e.g., "Integrity," "Innovation," "Collaboration").
- Alternatively, prepare value words on slips of paper or sticky notes.
- A large table or wall space for grouping and sorting values.

2. Materials for Remote Teams:

- Use a digital collaboration tool to create a virtual deck of value cards.
- Alternatively, use a slide deck or spreadsheet with value words listed.

- Ensure participants have access to a meeting platform with screen sharing and breakout rooms, if needed.

3. Explain the purpose of the activity and share any necessary instructions (e.g., how to interact with the cards physically or digitally).

Activity Steps

1. Value Exploration

- **In-person:** Distribute the value cards among participants or place them on a table.
- Ask each person to pick three to five cards that they feel are most important for the team or organization.
- **Remote:** Share a digital board or file with the value cards. Ask participants to drag and drop three to five cards into their personal workspace or write their selections in the chat.

2. Sharing and Grouping

- **In-person:** One by one, participants place their chosen cards on a shared surface (e.g., table or wall) and explain their choices.
- Group similar values together as they are shared, using sticky notes or labels to name clusters.
- **Remote:** Participants explain their choices to the group while dragging their selected cards onto a shared virtual board.
- Group similar values together on the board using virtual tools like labels, color coding, or grouping features.

3. Group Discussion and Refinement

- Facilitate a discussion about the grouped values, asking open-ended questions such as:
- Why are these values important for our team?
- How do these values currently show up in how we work?

- Are there any missing values that we should include?

4. Prioritizing Values

- **In-person:** Use tools like dot stickers, ranking, or open discussion to prioritize the values.
- **Remote:** Use virtual voting features, digital dot stickers, or polls to identify the top values.
- Categorize the values into three groups:
- **Core Values:** The team's non-negotiable guiding principles.
- **Important Values:** Strongly influential but secondary.
- **Aspirational Values:** Values the team wants to embody more fully.

5. Defining Values

- For the top-selected values, collaborate as a group to define what each value means in your specific context.
- Provide examples of how these values can be demonstrated in your team's day-to-day actions. For example, if "Transparency" is selected, a practical behavior might be, "We provide regular project updates during team meetings."

6. Define Boundaries by Identifying "Red Lines"

Defining what your team values is crucial, but it's equally important to be explicit about the behaviors or attitudes that contradict those values and undermine your team's purpose. This step focuses on defining the team's "Red Lines"—the specific values, attitudes, or behaviors that conflict with your core values and are unacceptable within the team. Clarifying these helps protect the team culture and reinforce the commitments made in the previous steps.

- **In-person:** Write these red lines on separate cards or sticky notes and place them next to the team's core values on a table or wall.
- Ask the group reflective questions such as:

- What values would undermine trust or collaboration within our team?

- Which attitudes are completely at odds with our core values?

- **Remote:** Use a dedicated section of your virtual board to list the team's **red lines** alongside the core values.

  - Facilitate a discussion with the same reflective questions:

  - What values would disrupt our team's alignment and purpose?

  - Are there any priorities that contradict the values we've identified?

Group Discussion:

- Reflect on how the red lines relate to your core values. For example, if "Respect" is a core value, a red line might be "Disrespectful communication."

- Ensure the team reaches consensus on these red lines and understands their importance in protecting the team's culture and identity.

Debrief

1. Summarize the Final Values and Red Lines

- Share the finalized list of **prioritized values** along with their agreed-upon definitions.

- Highlight the **Red Lines** the team has identified—values or attitudes that are not acceptable because they undermine the team's purpose and culture.

2. Discuss Application

- Talk about how these values and red lines can be embedded into team culture, workflows, and decision-making processes.

3. Set Actionable Next Steps

- Ensure alignment by deciding how to reinforce and uphold them in daily operations, such as during meetings or when resolving conflicts.

Follow-Up

1. **Create a Visual Representation:** Develop a poster, infographic, or digital graphic that showcases the team's values and their definitions. Display it in the office or share it in your team's virtual workspace.

2. **Embed in Culture:** Integrate values into performance reviews, onboarding, and recognition programs.

3. **Periodic Check-Ins:** Revisit the team's values and red lines quarterly or annually to ensure they remain relevant and are actively guiding the team's behavior.

While doing this exercise with the telecom HR transformation team they emphasized the need for an "information-sharing culture" as part of transparency. They found that effective HR transformation required open channels of communication, where information was accessible and decisions were clear to all. It wasn't just about breaking down silos but also about creating a unified "information field" across HR functions. This value of transparency was critical to building trust, especially in a company with such a large workforce, where communication breakdowns could lead to misinformation and resistance.

From Values to Norms: Turning Ideas into Action

Defining your team's values is only the beginning. The real impact will come when you translate those values into clear, observable behaviors. For each value that resonates with the team, ask: How does this value show up in our work? For example, if you're aligned around integrity, brainstorm behaviors that demonstrate integrity in action. Does it mean communicating transparently, owning up to mistakes, or something else entirely?

Values become powerful when they are tied to specific acts. Once the HR transformation team defined transparency as a core value, they went further to illustrate what it looked like in practice. They agreed that transparency in their context meant regular updates to stakeholders at every level—whether it was the leadership team, managers, or front-line employees. This would include setting up monthly "all-hands on deck" updates and creating easily accessible documentation for all HR initiatives.

The team recognized that achieving company-wide transformation in HR would require a shift from working in isolated functions to cross-functional teamwork. For this, they created a principle around "working towards a common goal." In practical terms, this behavior meant setting up cross-functional task forces to address specific HR challenges, like onboarding or employee well-being, where members from different HR departments would collaborate on solutions.

Create Team Norms

Team norms take values and behaviors a step further by providing a framework for decision-making. After the team agrees on core values, the next step is to create team norms that put those values into action and become almost a part of the muscle memory of the team culture. These norms should be specific enough to be useful yet flexible enough to apply to different scenarios.

In the case of a telecom HR transformation team I coached, they were wrestling with how to balance speed with quality when implementing HR initiatives. They knew they needed to respond quickly to business needs, but not at the expense of careful execution. To address this, we established a norm called "doing things the right way." Inspired by a shared desire for excellence, this principle was based on the idea that while speed was essential, quality control and attention to detail were of equal value. They further defined this principle by committing to piloting all major HR changes within a small group of employees before rolling them out company-wide, ensuring both quality and adaptability in their work.

When the Rubber Meets the Road

Once, a CEO and founder of a small manufacturing company invited me to help solve a growing problem. The company's C-suite was becoming fragmented, with leaders forming cliques and subgroups. These internal divides made decision-making slow and execution even slower. New initiatives stalled because they lacked the necessary support.

The frustrating part? Everyone genuinely wanted the company to succeed. They believed in its mission, but they lacked clear, agreed-upon norms for how the team should work together. This lack of alignment was holding them back from achieving their full potential.

During a leadership team session, I introduced an exercise to address the issue. First, we discussed the team's purpose and core values—what they wanted to stand for as a leadership team. Once we had that foundation, I asked them to go a step further: to define the behaviors they wanted to see more of in their team and those they absolutely would not tolerate.

We divided these into two categories: Keep It Up behaviors, the actions they wanted to encourage and reward, and Cut It Out behaviors, those they would no longer accept. For example, their Keep It Ups included things like:

- Responding to colleagues' requests within one day.
- Demonstrating honesty and openness in communication.
- Sharing best practices with one another.

Their Cut It Outs, on the other hand, included:

- Blaming others for mistakes.
- Failing to take responsibility for actions.
- Avoiding difficult conversations or sweeping problems under the rug.

The team fully embraced the exercise. By the end of the session, they had created a clear, actionable framework for how they would hold each other accountable and work together as a cohesive unit.

Six months later, the CEO called me to share an update. The team had made significant progress—conflicts were down, and strategic projects that had previously stalled were now moving forward. But the real breakthrough? The leadership team had decided to fire their VP of Sales.

Why? Because she repeatedly failed to demonstrate the agreed-upon Keep It Up behaviors and consistently violated the Cut It Outs. Despite multiple conversations, she continued to prioritize her personal interests over the team's goals and ignored the norms the team had established. What stood out most to the CEO was that this decision didn't come from him. It came from the team. They had reached a point where they were self-sufficient—confident in holding each other accountable to the norms they had created. Instead of waiting for the leader to step in, they took ownership of the decision because it was rooted in their shared agreements and commitment to the company's success.

This story is a powerful example of how establishing clear team norms—based on shared values—can transform a team. It creates alignment, fosters accountability, and empowers the team to make tough decisions, even without direct intervention from the leader.

WOW Moments

One of the Keep It Up behaviors that every team should have is WOW moments. We all love a bit of well-deserved celebration when we've done something great, don't we? It's not just a feel-good moment, though. It's also a great way to keep our teams feeling positive and motivated. Take a moment to think about it. When was the last time you truly paused to acknowledge a job well done? I bet those moments had a lovely ripple effect, didn't they? They probably gave you a boost of energy and also lifted the collective enthusiasm of your team.

We all know that work can be demanding, and it's so easy to get caught up in the next deadline that we forget to celebrate the milestones along the way. That's why it's so important to have these WOW Moments —they're intentional celebrations of achievements! They give everyone a chance to take a step back, reflect on all their hard work, and feel genuinely proud of everything they've done.

For instance, after launching a new app, a team might have a celebratory lunch or give awards to those who went above and beyond. I've seen this play out firsthand in my own projects, and it's been so inspiring! A simple, thoughtful celebration transformed the team's energy. Everyone left feeling really appreciated and recharged, ready to take on the next challenge with a new spring in their step!

Here's what I recommend:

1. Brainstorm Celebration Ideas Together

Bring the team together and ask: *What would make us feel celebrated?* Whether it's a team lunch, personalized thank-you notes, or a shout-out in a meeting, the best celebrations are the ones that resonate with your group.

2. Vote on the Most Popular Ideas

Once you've gathered ideas, let the team decide which celebrations feel most meaningful. This ensures everyone feels involved and excited about what's to come.

3. Make It a Habit

Don't wait for the "perfect" moment—celebrate both big wins and the small victories along the way. That consistency builds a sense of momentum and keeps everyone motivated.

Make it personal. Make it memorable. Make it a WOW Moment.

As we conclude this first section, we've learned about the potential in teams once they discover their purpose and do the work necessary to click. We've reflected on the potential of teamwork and how to create great teams that are really clicking together. Purpose answers the "why," values define "how," and norms outline "what we do together to fulfill our purpose." When all three align, your team operates with clarity, accountability, and momentum.

Teams that take the time to establish a statement of purpose, a constitution that lays out shared values coupled wit actionable norms so their workers experience fewer conflicts, are capable of faster decision-making and greater trust. They create a culture where everyone feels empowered to contribute, and tough decisions are made based on mutual agreements—not personal bias or guesswork.

By translating values into norms, your team moves from intention to action. This framework builds cohesion and fosters a sense of ownership that enables teams to thrive even in challenging situations. Now it's your turn. Start the conversation with your team and see how the clarity of shared purpose, values, and norms transforms the way you work together.

As we move into the next chapters, we'll uncover additional critical elements to help you transform your team into a true CLICK team.

PART 2

LINKING CONNECTIONS

"No man is an island, entire of itself; every man is a piece of the continent, a part of the main."

—John Donne (1572–1631), English poet and cleric

As we've seen, a CLICK team is not just a group of disconnected individuals working independently in silos. A real team works together—cohesively. A CLICK team works with understanding not only their own roles but the roles of every other member. CLICK team members ask themselves: How do I fulfill my role? How do I contribute to the bigger picture? How do my teammates support my mission—and how do I support theirs? And ultimately, how do we serve the organization's overarching goal?

If there is no collaboration, there is no team. Without collaboration, you cannot click. Clicking is about building strong, purposeful connections—organic and engaged collaboration between team members and the stakeholders who depend on their work. These relationships—this integrated and engaged network—form the backbone of a team and power a company's ability to deliver meaningful results and create lasting impact.

Far too often, teams focus only on internal dynamics, assuming the leader is solely responsible for managing external relationships. In reality, building a thriving team ecosystem is a shared responsibility. Every team member must answer one essential question: What purpose does this team serve, and why does this work matter? Without that clarity, teams can lose sight of their purpose and drift from the organization's broader objectives. The first step toward creating a mutually interdependent and cohesive ecosystem is breaking down the silos within the team and between the team and its stakeholders.

So, what does a strong Linking Connections look like? Internally, team members collaborate effectively, leveraging each other's strengths, picking each other up when they fall. Externally, they are proactive in building relationships within the wider organizational **ecosystem**. They are responsive, engaged, relevant and aligned with each other, and keep their broader organizational priorities in view.

In order to achieve this kind of synergy, you need to accomplish the following milestones:

1. Balance one-on-one interactions with team-wide communication.

2. Shift your team's mindset from working in isolation to working together with people outside the immediate team— stakeholders, internal partners, leadership team, etc.

3. Become a part of the ecosystem of teams within the organization.

Creating a CLICK ecosystem isn't just a nice-to-have; it's a critical business competency for leaders and teams that want to move beyond functioning to truly excelling. Building strong and cooperative internal and external relationships enables your team to maximize its impact in a culture of achievement and mutual support. Let's start down that road now by rethinking how your team connects, communicates, and collaborates, and then pull it all together into a perfectly harmonized and collaborative network.

CHAPTER 4

STRONG TEAMS ARE BUILT PEER-TO-PEER, NOT TOP-DOWN

One of the most common challenges I've seen in my coaching and consulting work with leaders is that despite their best efforts, they often unintentionally become a bottleneck, constricting rather than expanding collaboration.

You're likely already doing a lot of the right things already quite naturally, just because you are you, and because you have to do many of these things to be good at your job. You support your team members. You offer thoughtful coaching and constructive feedback and support. You make time for regular one-on-one meetings, ensuring that each person feels heard and valued. And, of course, you promote social activities and team-building events, hoping this kind of interaction will boost morale and foster stronger connections.

These are all excellent practices that are foundational to good leadership. There is, however, a critical piece that often gets overlooked. Many leaders neglect to foster peer-to-peer connections. These connections reduce the dependency on you as a leader and will ultimately save you time and energy. They are also the literal engine of innovation, efficiency, and team morale. When team members collaborate directly, they share their diverse perspectives, spark creative solutions together, and build trust in each other's abilities. Without this level of interconnection, teams often stagnate or rely too heavily on their manager or top leadership for guidance, decision-making, and problem solving.

When leaders overlook peer-to-peer connections, it sets the stage for a harmful dynamic creating teams that are overly reliant on the leader for guidance, answers, conflict resolution, etc. What happens when team members always come to you instead of working things out for themselves? Management becomes overwhelmed. Bandwidth, already stretched thin, becomes further compromised, leaving even less time to focus on the larger strategic initiatives. Meanwhile, team performance plateaus because they haven't developed the autonomy and interdependence to engine innovation and realize success on their own.

Research reveals that teams with high levels of interdependence perform better because an ecosystem encourages shared participation and productive collaboration. A meta-analysis of over 100 studies found that task and outcome interdependence significantly improve both team performance and relational dynamics. Teams thrive when their workflows require coordination and their rewards emphasize collective success. Interdependence creates a feedback loop of accountability and innovation. Members understand that their success is tied to the group's collective performance, which fosters a sense of ownership and mutual respect. In a CLICK ecosystem, teams don't need to wait for leadership to guide them— they're equipped to move forward together.

You Don't Have to Have a Hand in Every Pie

In my early years as a manager, I fell into a trap that might sound familiar. I wanted to be involved in everything. I attended every meeting my team held, whether with internal stakeholders or external partners. I was copied on every email, kept tabs on all ongoing projects, and made it my mission to know every detail in every silo, down to the last nut and bolt. It wasn't micromanagement in the traditional sense—I wasn't dictating my team's every move. Instead, I sought their input, listened to their ideas, and made them feel supported. But what I didn't do was step back and let them make mistakes, solve the problem together, learn from their mistakes, and take ownership of their decisions, and the consequences of those decisions.

I had unknowingly not only created but also become the bottleneck, blocking the agency and synergy of my team. My team relied on me for everything—guidance, decisions, and approvals. This dynamic overwhelmed me with tasks and information, leaving me unable to focus on the most important part of my role: managing external relationships and advocating for my team's broader impact. It also made my team feel less connected, less engaged, and less motivated to take on tasks and go for the win.

My eyes opened when I was discussing the results of the engagement survey with my manager. My team rated me very highly as a manager, but their engagement level was one of the lowest in the organization. I didn't know why or how to interpret those results. That's when my manager asked me—who is the most connected person on the team? And I realized it was me.

I had regular conversations with every team member, but they had far fewer connections because I was their go-to person for every question. My manager helped me realize that my primary responsibility wasn't to be the team's internal problem solver, but to position my team for success by enabling internal collaboration and representing their expertise externally. So, I stepped back. Slowly, intentionally, I let my team members take full ownership of the projects they were leading. That meant they were the ones going to senior leaders, asking questions, and presenting results. They started building relationships beyond me—grabbing lunch with new colleagues, making cross-functional connections, and becoming more visible across the organization.

Something shifted. As their engagement increased, so did the quality of their work. They designed better training courses—more relevant, more impactful—because they were closer to the employees and understood their real needs. And as a result, those employees felt seen, supported, and performed better.

That's the power of connection. When people are trusted to step into ownership and build their own networks, performance improves—but so does well-being. I saw it firsthand not only with my own team but later on with teams I coached. Interconnectedness isn't just a feel-good concept; it's a business imperative.

Moving from individual work to micro-collaborations

A project management team at a tech consulting firm I recently worked with was struggling after transitioning to remote work. In the office, they had been a tight-knit group, frequently exchanging ideas and collaborating naturally and informally. But when team meetings were whittled down to once a week and were replaced by one-on-ones with their manager, Tanya, all that great synergy and natural collaboration suddenly fell apart. Team members began to feel isolated, and Tanya, who wanted to position her group at the center of project management expertise in the company, was growing increasingly frustrated. She had talented people, but they weren't connecting in ways that could drive innovation or learning.

In a team session, people identified isolation as their primary challenge with working remotely. They wanted to learn from one another and share ideas, but their remote setup wasn't conducive to collaboration. Together, they implemented two key changes that completely transformed their dynamics and relieved the team's sense of isolation.

1. **Knowledge-Sharing Fridays:** Every Friday, one team member shared insights from their particular area of expertise. These sessions gave others a better understanding of the context behind their colleagues' work and sparked ideas for integrating those insights into their own projects. It also gave team members working remotely a little unstructured time to connect in fresh ways.

2. **Collaborative Pairing for Projects**: Instead of working solo on tasks within their individual specialties, team members started inviting others into their process and began working in pairs. That might seem like it increased the volume of work everyone was doing, but in reality, team members became more informed about each stage of the projects and started making quicker decisions, spending much less time discussing different options. They discovered that working together saved them time and effort.

Within three months, these small changes yielded remarkable results. No only the team become better in collaboration. They also emerged as the center of excellence for project management in the organization. Their unique blend of functional expertise, project management acumen, and their new collaborative skills earned them recognition across departments. They began sharing their approach with other teams, showcasing both their technical expertise and their innovative methods for teamwork and communication. They became a new model for remote team success.

Encourage your team to seek out each other's expertise first. When challenges arise, their default shouldn't be to come to you but to collaborate with a teammate. Together, they can brainstorm, devise solutions, and move forward. If they need your approval, great. If not, they're empowered to execute without delay.

Overcoming an Action Bias

When we examine the core functions of any team, we find they engage in four primary activities:

- **Ideation** - This is the process where teams generate new ideas and solutions. It is a critical phase for innovation and creativity within teams.

- **Planning** - Planning involves setting goals and outlining the steps necessary to achieve them. It is crucial for organizing team efforts and ensuring that all members are aligned with the team's objectives.

- **Execution** - This is the phase where teams implement their plans and carry out tasks. Execution is often the most time-consuming activity as it involves the actual work needed to achieve the team's goals.

- **Reflection** - After execution, teams engage in reflection to assess their performance and identify areas for improvement. This process is vital for learning and adapting to new challenges, and it can significantly enhance future team performance.

In practice, teams often spend the majority of their time on execution, followed by planning, ideation, and finally reflection and improvement. This focus on execution happens because teams face immediate demands to complete tasks and often prioritize short-term goals over long-term development.

This imbalance holds teams back. A Singapore Management University study[9] found that dedicating more time to reflection and learning creates a deeper learning experience, fosters a positive team atmosphere, and enhances coordination. In other words, investing in activities like planning and reflection pays off in the form of improved team performance and stronger relationships over time.

The study highlights the downside of neglecting these phases: Teams tend to exhibit an "action bias," prioritizing task completion over learning and reflection, and long-term success. This bias limits their ability to adapt, address failures, and improve processes. On the other hand, formalizing time for reflection counters this bias, enabling teams to analyze their behavior, plan better, develop long vision and achieve greater gains.

So how do you counteract this imbalance and promote peer-to-peer connection and a focus on the future? Start by intentionally creating opportunities for your team to share knowledge and reflect. You could pair less experienced members with seasoned teammates for mentorship. Host regular learning sessions where individuals share insights, new skills, or lessons from recent projects. Or introduce creative activities like a "Failure Party" [10]to celebrate mistakes and reflect on what the team has learned.

---

[9]   Goh, Kenneth & Fisher, Colin & Sommer, S.. (2022). The Effect of Formal Time Allocations on Learning Trajectories and Performance. Small Group Research. 53. 104649642210923. 10.1177/10464964221092331.

[10]   Read more about Failure Party here https://dariarudnik.com/tpost/rvnh519jr1-why-your-team-needs-a-failure-party-yes

Inspire Agency in Micro-Groups

Leaders have the tendency to want to step in and solve every issue, rather than letting their teams work through their own process independently—or in smaller subgroups—and come up with solutions on their own. Rather than stepping in to solve every issue, ask your team to collaborate with one another, and then and only then, ask them to present their findings or proposed solutions to you. Not only does this approach empower your team members, but it also fosters a sense of ownership and accountability while strengthening the bonds between team members.

You've probably heard the famous management mantra: *"Don't bring me problems—bring me solutions."* While this can encourage accountability and critical thinking, it's not a one-size-fits-all rule. There will be times when your team members may struggle to develop a solution—perhaps due to limited resources, insufficient knowledge, or a lack of expertise. And that's okay. But they certainly aren't going to get any better at coming up with solutions independently if you never give them the chance.

Instead of demanding fully-formed solutions, establish a new norm: Ask them to address the situation with their peers first BEFORE bringing a problem to you. Whether they come to you with a proposed solution, a deeper understanding of the challenge, or just a list of clarifying questions, the key is that they've already leveraged the collective brainpower of the team in advance. And they will get better over time. This process ensures that collaboration happens first and that no one person shoulders the burden of solving complex problems alone.

This doesn't mean you're stepping away from problem-solving entirely. It's about recognizing that many of the people on your team have specific expertise that surpasses your own in certain areas—and encouraging them to use that expertise collaboratively. Not only does this make your team more effective, but it also creates opportunities for them to rely on each other, leverages talent, builds trust and strengthens connections across the group.

By requiring your team to engage with one another before coming to you, you're doing more than just delegating problem-solving. You're creating an interconnected network where individuals feel accountable not only to you but also to each other and seek out opportunities to shine. In doing so, you're also instilling a sense of agency, creativity, and growth. That sense of interdependence is a hallmark of high-performing teams and a critical step in building an authentic CLICK team.

Building interconnected cultures

The nature of work in organisations requires teams need to collaborate and seek input on decisions from various people outside their immediate team. Being able to communicate with them directly empowers your team members and also provides them with the critical information they need to reach their goals.

Encourage them to present their solutions in meetings rather than relying on you as the go-between. Let them go to their peers in other departments for information and meaningful input. Not only does this build their confidence, but it also frees you from being the perpetual middleman.

Over time, these direct interactions will make your team more agile and self-reliant. They'll develop the capability to navigate relationships, solve problems, and drive projects forward without needing your constant involvement. That independence doesn't just lighten your workload—it amplifies your team's impact and credibility across the organization.

Ultimately, the role of a leader in a high-performing team isn't to be the sole problem solver or decision-maker. It's to create an environment where team members feel empowered to rely on each other, and together, push the team forward.

By taking these steps—encouraging collaboration in micro-groups, spending more time on reflection, and letting team members build strong connections outside your team—you'll not only free yourself from the constant pressure of being the go-to person on every task but also unlock your team to tap into their own agency, creativity, and self-reliance.

You might be wondering—*if I'm not the one solving all the problems or guiding my team through every stakeholder interaction, what's my role as a leader? Why do they even need me?*

And honestly, that's a great question to ask. I've had this conversation with many of the leaders I've coached, and one response really stood out to me. *"My role as a leader is to create the space for my team to grow and thrive. I do this by building an environment where they feel supported by me and their teammates. I create a culture, where people feel able to take ambitious action, where it's okay to make mistakes —and, more importantly, where we can openly share those mistakes and learn from them."*

That's such a powerful way to look at leadership. It shifts the focus from managing every detail to cultivating an environment where your team can flourish and manage the details on their own. This is the role of a CLICK leader.

To create this kind of space, you need to do two key things: Build stronger connections between team members and help them build connections with colleagues and teams outside of your team. By doing so, you're not just enabling your team to rely on each other internally, but you're also empowering them to interact directly with external partners, present their ideas, and solve challenges without requiring you to be the middleman.

In this model, your role evolves. You're no longer the bottleneck; instead, you're the facilitator of growth, trust, and collaboration—both within the team and beyond. And that's where your leadership truly makes an impact.

Checklist For Leaders: Are You Spending Too Much Time on 1:1s?

One of the greatest leadership tools of all time is 1:1s. It's the time when a leader and team member can focus on the team member's development and when the leader can learn about their challenges and aspirations. But sometimes leaders forget that 1:1s are just one of the tools in their toolkit. There are other less labor intensive options at your disposal.

When you have eight people on your team, having weekly 1:1s takes up a huge amount of your time. Even eight biweekly meetings can be very challenging, given everything else on your plate. And to be honest—you don't need that many meetings to build relationships and discuss development plans. At a certain point, it becomes an exercise in diminishing returns to status update with each and every one of your reports all the time. It creates a traffic jam.

If you're wondering whether you've unintentionally become a bottleneck for your team, this checklist can provide valuable clarity. It's designed to help leaders evaluate how their approach to communication, particularly 1:1 meetings, may be hindering rather than helping team-wide collaboration. By assessing your time allocation and the dynamics within your team, you can identify opportunities to shift from being the center of all decision-making to empowering your team to solve problems collectively, and with fewer meetings.

This checklist has helped dozens of leaders rethink their communication with team members and build more interconnected teams. Use it to assess whether your time spent in 1:1s—whether scheduled or ad hoc—is limiting your ability to foster team-wide collaboration and build stronger peer-to-peer connections.

For each question, rate your agreement on a 5-point scale:

1 = **Fully Disagree**

2 = **Disagree**

3 = **Neutral**

4 = **Agree**

5 = **Fully Agree**

The "Am I Holding Too Many Meetings" Self Check

1. Are individual meetings dominating your calendar?

Do you spend more than 50% of your time in 1:1s, leaving little room for team-wide activities, collaboration, or strategic thinking?

2. Are you repeating the same topics across multiple 1:1s?

Do you find yourself discussing similar issues or giving the same guidance to different team members instead of addressing these in a group setting?

3. Do team members primarily come to you for answers instead of collaborating with each other?

Are they relying on you as the main problem solver for issues that could be better addressed through peer collaboration?

4. Do you feel like a bottleneck for decision-making?

Are you slowing the team's ability to act independently because they seek your input too often?

5. Is there limited peer-to-peer interaction on your team?

Do individuals bypass their colleagues and approach you directly for feedback, approvals, or support instead of leveraging their teammates' expertise?

6. Do hybrid or remote team members struggle to connect with one another?

In a hybrid or remote work setting, do team members lack opportunities to collaborate, share knowledge, or form connections independently of you?

Scoring and Action Plan

Once you've answered all the questions, calculate your score by adding up your responses for all six questions. A **lower score** reflects a healthier balance between 1:1s and team-wide collaboration, while a **higher score** indicates potential areas for improvement.

6–12: High Collaboration and Self-Sufficiency

- **What This Means:** Your team is highly collaborative and self-reliant. They solve problems independently, collaborate effectively, and leverage each other's strengths without over-relying on you.

- **Action Steps:**
  - Maintain this balance by regularly reinforcing team dynamics through collaborative projects and celebrations of success.
  - Focus on fine-tuning smaller areas like innovation, stakeholder engagement, or refining decision-making processes.

13–18: Balanced, But Opportunities for Improvement

- **What This Means:** You're striking a reasonable balance, but there are areas where your reliance on 1:1s may be limiting peer-to-peer collaboration. Your team might still look to you as a central figure for decision-making.

- **Action Steps:**
  - Consolidate repetitive 1:1 topics into group discussions.
  - Facilitate peer-to-peer problem-solving by assigning group-based tasks or decision-making opportunities.
  - Identify specific areas where the team can grow in autonomy and collaboration.

19–30: Reliance on 1:1s Is Hindering Team Collaboration

- **What This Means:** You may be over-relying on individual meetings, which could be limiting your team's growth, collaboration, and independence. This may result in inefficiencies and bottlenecks.

- **Action Steps:**
  - Restructure your approach to focus more on team-wide discussions and shared responsibilities.
  - Encourage your team to engage with one another first before seeking your input.
  - Build systems or processes for recurring topics to reduce the need for individual meetings.

Every team is unique. The ideal balance between 1:1s and team-wide communication depends on your team's size, culture, and dynamics. In hybrid and remote settings, fostering connectivity requires intentional effort to ensure everyone feels included and aligned.

By using this checklist as a starting point, you can identify areas for improvement and build a more interconnected, self-sufficient team.

CHAPTER 5

THINK LIKE A NETWORK, NOT A HIERARCHY

In any organizational setting, you'll rarely work in isolation. Your team's efforts will almost always ripple outward, affecting multiple stakeholders. To ensure your work gains the support it needs and delivers the expected results, it's essential to identify these stakeholder groups, understand the influence they wield, and consider their critical role in shaping the purpose of your team in addition to the broader organization.

Let's break this down into four key stakeholder groups and how you can effectively engage with each.

1. **Internal Partners**

Think of internal partners as your inner circle—your team members and close organizational allies and critical components of your ecosystem, who help drive your goals forward. Depending on your team's structure, this might also involve individuals from other departments or divisions who collaborate closely with you on projects. These partners bring a mix of skills, expertise, and perspectives that are vital to your team's success.

If your team operates in a highly specialized capacity and doesn't often work with others, your internal partners might be limited to your immediate team. In many cases, however, you'll find yourself working hand-in-hand with other units. When that happens, it's important to include them in your list of internal partners.

To make the most of these relationships, focus on establishing clear communication channels, defining roles and responsibilities, and fostering a collaborative environment. When you understand their unique contributions and address their needs, you'll unlock their full potential and drive your projects forward.

2. External Partners

External partners are your outside partners: vendors, contractors, consultants, service providers, or even strategic partners who bring specialized expertise, resources, or services to the table. Their role is often to fill gaps in your team's capabilities or to provide critical deliverables that you can't produce internally.

Building strong relationships with external partners requires clear communication and alignment of goals. Start by identifying their expectations and establishing formal agreements, such as contracts or service-level agreements, to ensure everyone is on the same page. When you foster trust and collaboration with these external partners, you'll create a seamless integration of efforts that drives success.

3. Decision-makers and Influencers

Decision-makers and influencers hold the keys to your project's success. These include senior management, executives, or key stakeholders who control resources, make strategic decisions, or influence the broader organizational priorities. Their support can make or break your project, so it's crucial to understand their goals, concerns, and expectations and figure out ways to work collaboratively to meet those goals.

Engage with decision-makers and influencers regularly. Keep them informed with updates that highlight your project's value and address any risks or challenges. Involve them in key decisions and seek their input to ensure alignment. When you actively demonstrate how your work supports their priorities, you'll secure their commitment and create a smoother path to success.

4. **End-users or Beneficiaries**

At the heart of every project are the people who will ultimately use or benefit from your work. End-users or beneficiaries might be customers, employees, or community members. Their needs and expectations should guide your decisions and shape your outcomes.

Engage with this group early and often. Use tools like surveys, focus groups, or user testing to gather feedback and incorporate their insights into your work. Their insights are gold—use them to refine and improve your solutions.

Mapping Your Stakeholders

Stakeholder groups can have diverse interests, ranging from a direct interest in your work to those who are indirectly affected but still important. When identifying stakeholders, aim to be intuitive and adaptable. Consider their roles, perspectives, and the potential risks or benefits they bring to the table. Walk a mile in their shoes. It's better to include as many people as you can remember and then adjust the list. There's no harm in adding an extra person—but missing someone important can put your whole career at risk.

Remember, stakeholders also have their own networks of secondary stakeholders. Take the time to understand these extended connections and how they might influence your work. By creating a comprehensive stakeholder map tailored to your project and organization, you'll be better equipped to navigate relationships, anticipate challenges, read others intentions and agendas, and drive your team toward success.

As you move forward, keep this in mind: The strength of your team's connections—both within and beyond the organization—will determine your ability to deliver impactful results. By understanding and engaging your stakeholders effectively, you'll not only gain the support you need but also create a foundation for long-term success.

The Apple of Discord: A Tale for Stakeholder Inclusion

One of my favorite Greek myths is the story of the Apple of Discord. It happened at the wedding of the mortal Peleus and the sea nymph Thetis. It was one of the most celebrated events in all of Ancient Greece as these two would later give birth to the legendary Achilles. Every immortal was invited... well, almost everyone.

Eris, the goddess of strife, found herself without an invitation. You might say they had a good reason for not inviting her—after all, she was the goddess of discord, and wherever she went, trouble followed. But ignoring someone as powerful as her led to multiple disasters that affected many people and gods.

Eris did come to the wedding. Furious at being excluded, she tossed a golden apple inscribed with "To the Fairest" into the gathering. The resulting chaos was spectacular. Three powerful goddesses—Hera, Athena, and Aphrodite—each claimed the apple. Their rivalry escalated, drawing in mortals and gods alike, which, after many consequent events, ultimately led to the Trojan War—a conflict that reshaped the ancient world. All because one stakeholder was left off the invite list.

I've watched this Greek drama play out in many organizations I've worked with or for. The CFO is left out of purchasing decisions. IT rolls out a new system without consulting the security team. A product team launches a feature without involving customer support. And what happens? Carnage.

So, what's the best way to manage these situations? Here's a step-by-step guide on how to map all your stakeholders and manage them accordingly, making sure each and every one of them feels like the fairest of all.

Step 1: Identify All Relevant Stakeholders (Across the Four Groups)

Think about the different groups, individuals, or organizations that are relevant to your project or team. Write down everyone—especially those who enjoy tossing apples. Missing a key stakeholder can lead to unintended consequences, so be thorough in your assessment.

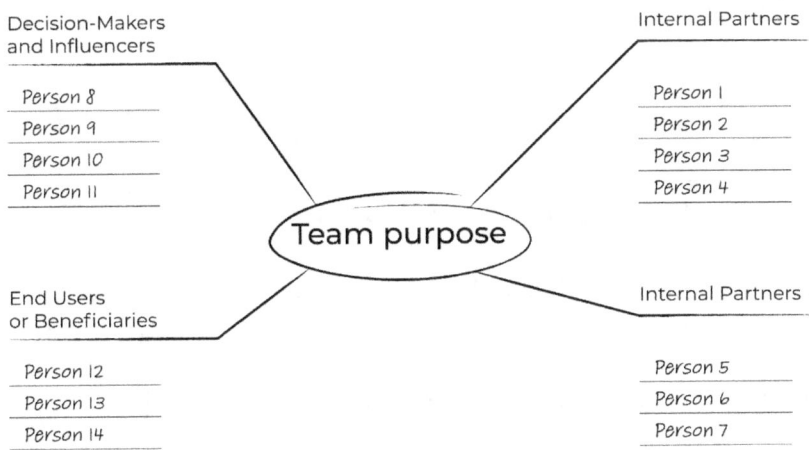

Step 2: Mark Their Level of Influence

Assess the influence each stakeholder has over your project or team. Put a "!" next to those stakeholders who have a high level of influence. These individuals or groups can make or break your project, so it's crucial to keep them informed and engaged.

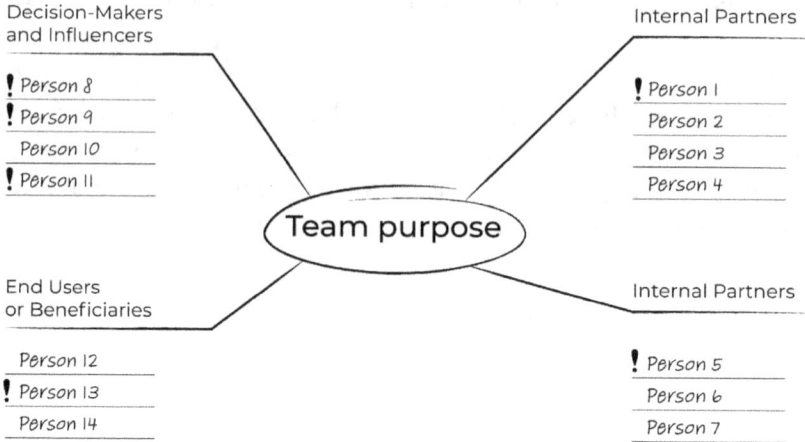

Step 3: Identify Supporters and Opponents

Put a "√" next to stakeholders who are strong supporters. Put an "X" next to stakeholders who are opponents. Supporters can help you gain traction and momentum, while opponents may create roadblocks. Understanding where each stakeholder stands allows you to strategize accordingly.

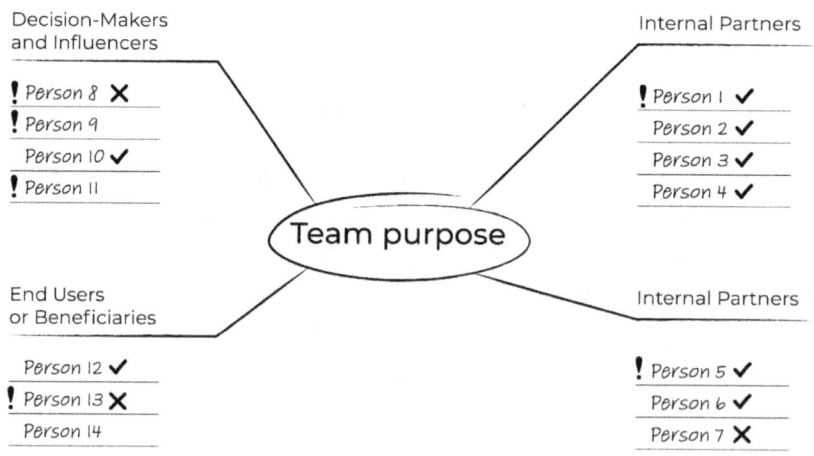

Step 4: Draw Connections Between Stakeholders

Draw a solid line between stakeholders who have strong relationships or interactions with each other. Draw a dashed line between stakeholders who have weak or less direct relationships. This helps you understand influence patterns and potential allies who can help you navigate challenges more effectively.

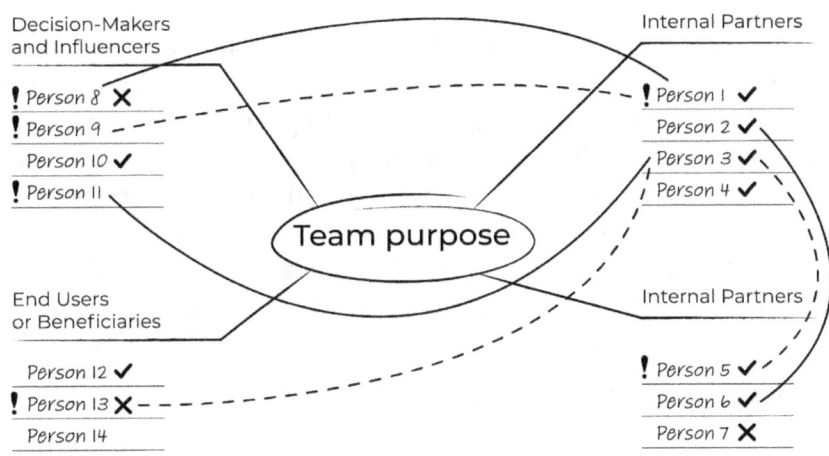

Step 5: Create a Communication Plan

Your top priority should be stakeholders from any of the four groups who have "!" high influence and who are "X" opponents. These individuals are in your "Danger Zone," meaning that they have both the will and power to prevent you from reaching your goals. Your primary goal in communicating with these folks is to neutralize their negativity. They don't need to become your strongest supporters (though it can happen), but they must in any event not stand in your way.

Your second priority includes stakeholders with "!" high influence who are also "✓" strong supporters—these individuals are in the "Green Zone." Ensure that these individuals continue to receive what they need from you so they remain engaged and supportive.

Your third priority consists of low-influence supporters. While these individuals may not hold much power on their own, collectively they can form a strong base of advocates in the "Support Zone." Over time, their backing can help shift organizational perspectives.

Finally, there are low-influence opponents in the "Monitor Zone." Your role here is to observe them closely—some may eventually become supporters if they see your "Support Zone" growing, while others may gain influence and move into the "Danger Zone."

Every plan needs not only a clear "what to do" but also "who will do it." Step 4's stakeholder connections will help determine this. Communication should not be based on hierarchy but on existing relationships and potential connections. As a leader, you don't need to manage every stakeholder yourself. Your team members can take ownership of relationships with key decision-makers, external partners, and end users. You might even find that some of them already have relationships in place. If not, it's a signal that your team is too disconnected from the rest of the organization.

Breaking Through the Wall

Sarah, head of the Cybersecurity team at FastGrowingCompany Inc., was staring at the results of the latest employee engagement survey. No surprises—her team scored the lowest in the company. It only confirmed what she had already felt. Her team was unmotivated, disconnected, and just going through the motions.

This didn't make sense to Sarah. She had always thought of herself as a good manager. She cared about her team. She shielded them from unpleasant conversations and feedback she felt was irrelevant or potentially hurtful. She held regular team meetings and 1:1s, always making sure everyone felt heard. On the surface, her team members seemed to appreciate her efforts and liked Sarah very much.

So why didn't they seem to care about their work?

Frustrated, Sarah dug deeper, analyzing every data point. And then she saw it—Organizational Network Analysis—a visual representation of how communication flows in the company, who is connected to whom, and how strong those connections are.

The map revealed the answer to Sarah's question: while all other teams were interconnected and were forming a dense network of collaboration, the Cybersecurity group sat at the very edge—all by itself, barely linked to anyone at all.

All the team communications were handled through Sarah. And although she did pass along important information, clearly it hadn't been enough for her team to truly feel they were part of a bigger organization. And then it clicked. Sarah hadn't been protecting her team members by shielding them from difficult feedback—she had been isolating them all.

By filtering stakeholder conversations, by acting as a gatekeeper and a shield, she had unknowingly cut her team off from the very people they were meant to serve. Without direct exposure to those stakeholders, her team had no real sense of why their work mattered or how it fit into the bigger picture.

No wonder they felt disengaged. No wonder their energy was fading. They needed to be reconnected to the vibrant ecosystem. Sarah exhaled slowly. This changed everything. Determined to turn things around, she called a meeting. It was time to map out their stakeholders properly—make them more than just names on a list, but real people, with whom real relationships needed to be built. Her team had to understand who relied on their work, what those people needed, and how to collaborate more effectively. And most importantly, they had to step out of their silo and connect with the rest of the organization. They had to leave the cocoon Sarah had spun around them all. And she had to trust them to be able to handle this new visibility—to take ownership of their work, their relationships, and their growth.

Sarah realized this wasn't just about boosting engagement scores. It was about making sure her team wasn't working in the dark anymore, getting clarity on bigger organizational goals, receiving feedback both positive and negative. And she had to trust them to be able to handle this new visibility—to take ownership of their work, their relationships, and their growth.

Breaking the Old Habit

Sarah's first instinct was to handle the stakeholder conversations herself—just as she always had. It was second nature by now. For years, she had acted as the gatekeeper, filtering external interactions so her team could stay focused on their technical tasks and not worry about the chatter. It felt like the most efficient way to operate.

But now, looking at the big picture, she saw the flaw in that approach.

If she truly wanted her team to feel connected and engaged, they had to be part of these conversations—not just hear about them secondhand once Sarah put them through her own filter. Shielding them from external discussions wasn't helping; it was holding them back.

She caught herself before falling into the old pattern. This time, she wouldn't take it all on alone. Instead, she gathered her team and laid out the plan.

Rather than dictating how things should go, Sarah turned the process into a collaborative team effort. Together, they mapped out key stakeholders and discussed who would be the best fit for each conversation. They considered existing relationships, areas of expertise, and the specific needs of each stakeholder.

Together they agreed that some discussions—particularly with high-influence stakeholders or those with complex needs—would still fall under Sarah's purview. But many others? They were better handled by the team independently of Sarah.

John, who had worked closely with the IT department on past security initiatives, took ownership of building the relationship with IT. His familiarity with their systems and challenges made him the perfect bridge. Meanwhile, Maria, who had a keen understanding of user experience and strong rapport with the Product team, stepped up to ensure cybersecurity was seamlessly integrated into development.

For the first time, the Cybersecurity team wasn't just reacting to external needs—they were actively shaping conversations and building stronger ties across the organization. As Sarah watched her team step into their appropriate roles and begin functioning autonomously, she realized something else: They were ready for the next step.

Stakeholder Engagement Questionnaire

To ensure that these conversations were productive and consistent, Sarah introduced the **Stakeholder Engagement Questionnaire.** This tool would guide each team member in their discussions, helping them gather important information and align on expectations.

Here's how Sarah and her team used the questionnaire:

Understanding and Expectations

Questions:

- On a scale of 1-10 (with 1 being worst and 10 being best), how clear are you about our team's vision and strategic goals?
- How aligned do you feel your interests and objectives are with our team's goals?
- What do you see as the key outcomes of our team's success for you or your organization?

How They Used It: John started his conversation with the IT department by asking these questions to gauge their understanding of the Cybersecurity team's goals. He discovered that while the IT team generally understood the importance of cybersecurity, they felt that the current protocols were out of step with their need for agility. This insight was critical for John to address in the ongoing collaboration.

Communication and Collaboration

Questions:

- On a scale of 1-10 (with 1 being worst and 10 being best), how would you rate the quality of communication between our team and you/your organization?

- How would you rate the level of collaboration between our team and you/your organization?

How They Used It: Maria used these questions in her discussion with the Product team. She learned that while they appreciated the security measures, they often felt that cybersecurity was an afterthought in the product development process. This feedback allowed Maria to propose more integrated security planning sessions early in the product lifecycle.

Feedback and Suggestions

Questions:

- Do you have any suggestions for how our team could better communicate or collaborate with you/your organization?

- Are there any potential obstacles or issues that you think we should be aware of as we pursue our strategic goals?

- Is there anything else you would like to share or discuss with our team?

How They Used It: Sarah herself took on the conversation with Legal. Through these questions, she found out that the Legal team often felt out of the loop on new cybersecurity protocols, which delayed contract negotiations. By addressing this, Sarah was able to establish a more streamlined process for keeping Legal informed, reducing delays and improving overall efficiency.

Empowering the Team

As Sarah's team stepped into their new roles, something remarkable happened. By sharing the responsibility of stakeholder engagement, Sarah wasn't just improving communication—she was shifting the entire team's mindset. No longer were they just technical experts working in the background. Now, they saw how their work fit into the larger ecosystem, how cybersecurity wasn't just a function but a vital part of the company's success They saw why their work and their role mattered, how they had been contributing to something larger than themselves.

Each team member returned from their stakeholder conversations with new insight and solutions they could immediately apply to their work. Security measures that once felt like isolated tasks now had clear context. Their contributions felt more meaningful, more aligned with the organization's needs. They felt more valuable and useful to the whole organization.

And it wasn't just the Cybersecurity team that benefitted.

Other departments, once disconnected from the team's mission, started to see them differently. Stakeholders appreciated the direct engagement, the opportunity to collaborate rather than just be handed policies to follow. The walls between teams weren't just coming down—they were being replaced with real partnerships.

Sarah knew this wasn't a one-time fix. Real engagement meant ongoing conversations, continuous learning, and regular check-ins to refine their approach. Together, they committed to making stakeholder engagement a permanent part of their strategy, using feedback to constantly improve and continuously adapt while strengthening connections across the company.

By taking these steps, Sarah didn't just solve an engagement problem—she transformed her team. The Cybersecurity group was no longer an isolated unit, but an integral, high-performing force within FastGrowingCompany Inc. And for the first time in a long time, Sarah could see it. They weren't just working. They were thriving.

Sarah's story reminds us to ditch the hierarchy and focus on value creation. If your team members are directly involved in creating value for a senior leader, they need to be part of the conversation.

A recruiter looking for a personal assistant to the CEO doesn't need the Chief People Officer or VP of Talent Acquisition as a middleman. A data analyst preparing insights for the CFO should be able to present their findings directly. A legal expert advising on compliance for the COO should be in the room when decisions are made.

Let the experts do the work you hired them to do. When you remove unnecessary barriers, teams move faster, communicate better, and create real impact. By connecting team members with people outside their immediate team—such as partners, internal clients, or internal providers—you strengthen the organizational ecosystem, making it more resilient and adaptive.

Similar to neural pathways in the brain, rarely used muscles tend to weaken, while those that are used frequently become stronger and more agile over time. The more we make use of our integrated neural networks, the better we're able to solve complex challenges and adapt—the same holds true for organizations, which thrive when rich, cross-functional connections are developed and then nurtured.

CHAPTER 6

NO TEAM IS AN ISLAND: BUILD YOUR ECOSYSTEM

No team in an organization exists as a single unit. In this chapter, we will explore how to build and support connections between multiple teams. These could be two teams within a larger unit or two separate teams that need to work closely together to fulfill their team purposes and contribute to a bigger organizational purpose.

CLICK teams create an ecosystem where they work collaboratively toward shared organizational goals. When Clear Purpose and Linking Connections are working well, an organization becomes a self-sustaining system that supports and fosters dynamic and organic growth. The culture transforms from organizational silos—where each function operates like a deep well protecting its water from others—into a connected and collaborative ecosystem.

It's natural for us as humans to seek out connection, and we also tend to gravitate toward those who are most like us. It's comfortable, it's easy. However, in a team setting, that comfort can cost us by lacking cohesion, collaboration, and, ultimately, performance.

When leading a larger team, you may notice that some parts of your team are more connected than others. At times, these groups may even exclude others. Such dynamics form naturally. People often bond based on shared interests, backgrounds, or workspaces. Sometimes colleagues from one office or location communicate more with each other than with those in a different region. Other times, a group working on specific tasks develops its own micro-culture.

Many of my clients who have experienced organizational changes have found themselves leading teams merged from different departments, struggling to find common ground and collaborate in a new setting. Whatever the case might be, if left unchecked, these divisions can lead to friction, misunderstanding, and resentment—ultimately hindering teamwork and productivity.

Creating Space for Collaboration

I remember being the Chief People Officer at a RetailTech company when I found myself constantly managing conflicts between two of my teams. The HR Administration team was at odds with the Talent Acquisition team. Despite sharing the same office space and working closely together, there was constant blame-shifting. The HR Admin team accused Talent Acquisition of not following procedures, leading to an increased workload and stressful friction over meeting the company's expectations for candidate and employee experience. On the flip side, Talent Acquisition blamed HR Admin for being too rigid and unwilling to adapt to candidates' and hiring managers' needs regarding process speed.

All my efforts to remind both teams that we shared a common goal—finding, hiring, and retaining the best talent—were in vain. All they could focus on were the goals of their own unit. Making sure all the documents were properly prepared, according to procedure and without mistakes, was the main focus for the HR Admin. Closing the vacancy as quickly as possible was the top priority for Talent Acquisition. And both teams seemed determined to diminish the other's goal, thinking their own mission was more important for the whole HR team and the organization in general.

When I heard them arguing, it hit me: I thought of the HR unit as a single team. But in reality, we were much more layered than this. We were an ecosystem of teams—HR Admin, Talent Acquisition, Learning and Development, Office Administration, etc. Each team had its own understanding of how their work contributed to the bigger HR and organizational goals. In order for all the teams to be able to collaborate, they needed to understand and align with each other's goals, processes, and ways of communication. So before trying to blend them into one unit, I needed to create a space for collaboration among these teams. And for that, we had to be crystal clear on:

- The value each team provides and how each team sees its role in the ecosystem of teams
- What outcomes they produce and who uses those outcomes
- What they need from other teams to create the value they aim to deliver and produce the outcomes others expect from them

When there is this clarity, teams start to see beyond their scope and see how they are a part of a bigger, more complex process and where their contribution is needed the most.

And here's how you can do the same.

Team Alignment Map

The Team Alignment Map visualizes each team's processes, tension points, and opportunities for better collaboration. It helps teams clarify their responsibilities and align expectations with other teams. It ensures that teams understand:

1. The value they create and their key deliverables
2. What they need from other teams to do their job effectively
3. What other teams expect from them and how to manage those expectations

This activity is particularly useful for breaking down silos, reducing miscommunication, and fostering cross-team collaboration in organizations where departments or units operate in isolation.

Why This Activity Is Effective

- Clarifies Responsibilities – Each team understands what they contribute and what others expect from them.
- Improves Cross-Team Collaboration – Helps teams identify misalignments, set clear expectations, and prevent misunderstandings.
- Breaks Down Silos – Encourages teams to interact beyond their usual group and work together more openly.

Equipment Needed

For Online Execution:

- Digital collaboration tools (Miro, MURAL, Notion)
- Virtual meeting platform (Zoom, Microsoft Teams, Google Meet)

For Offline Execution:

- Whiteboard or flipchart
- Sticky notes and markers

Preparation

1. Set Up the Team Alignment Map – Prepare a structured template with three sections:

   - What is our role and what value do we create?
   - What are our key outputs and deliverables?
   - What do we need from other teams to be successful?

2. Prepare Digital or Physical Materials – Ensure teams have access to collaboration tools or physical sticky notes.

3. Assign Teams – Each team, unit, or department participates to improve collaboration.

How to Conduct the Activity

Part 1: Define Each Team's Role in the Process

1. Define the Team's Value – Each team describes what they do, why their work matters, and how it impacts the organization.

2. Outline Outputs and Deliverables – Teams clarify what they produce and who depends on their work.

3. Identify Inputs – Each team lists what they need from other teams to work effectively.

Part 2: Align Expectations Between Teams

1. Teams Present Their Needs and Expectations – Each team shares with other teams what they expect to receive and what they will provide in return.

2. Review and Accept Expectations – Teams look at each other's expectations. Some of them are familiar to them; some might seem new. They also look at what the other team provides as an output and what other units in organizations expect from that. This creates a more holistic view of the process where those teams not only interact with each other but also provide value further in the organizations. And some of the reviewed expectations will be mutually agreed upon and integrated into the workflow while others might need further discussion.

3. Address Unresolved Expectations–Teams schedule follow-up meetings to discuss and negotiate solutions for any expectations they cannot immediately accept.

Input	HR Admin	Output
What do we need from other teams to be successful?	What is our role, and what value do we create?	What are our key outputs and deliverables?
Candidate CV & profile	We ensure the correct and timely processing of new employees, ensuring that all documentation complies with company requirements and legal regulations	Employment contract signed and stored
Complete candidate document package		Candidate fully registered in the internal staffing system
Signed offer		
Start date confirmation		IT Department request submitted for laptop, email, system access setup

The Team Alignment Map is a powerful tool for improving collaboration, ensuring clear expectations between teams, and breaking down organizational silos. By mapping out workflows, clarifying dependencies, and negotiating expectations, teams can work more efficiently, reduce friction, and build stronger relationships across teams, and the entire company.

Prioritize the Team of Peers

Another way to foster alignment among your teams is to ensure that all team members prioritize the team they are part of – Peer team – over the team they lead – Top-down team.

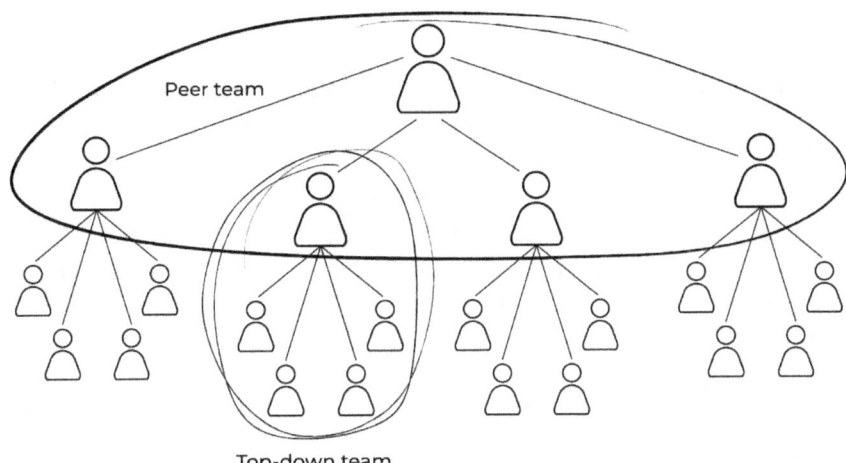

Peer team

Top-down team

A simple way to understand where they see themselves is to ask them: Which team is your priority? Or even—what is your team?

When I do this exercise with clients, over 90% of leaders prioritize the team they lead over the one they're part of. And it's no surprise why:

1. It's more beneficial for our ego to prioritize our leadership position over being someone else's follower.

2. Most leadership literature focuses on how to be a great leader, not on how to be a good follower or team member.

My good friend Dr. David Leitner, a followership and strategy specialist, often emphasizes a critical insight: Followership is not merely about compliance. Instead, it's a decision—a choice to actively participate in advancing someone else's vision and purpose. To join a strategic process guided by someone else. This choice isn't passive; it's about evangelism—inspired followers actively support and bolster that vision and process, often elevating it beyond its original scope.

To be effective, leadership must create the conditions for people to willingly and enthusiastically embrace followership. That means opening the door for them to see themselves not as subordinates but as strategic partners.

When done right, followership isn't just about "doing what you're told." It's about engaging as a strategic contributor, acting with integrity and agency, and finding ways to enhance the organization's mission. Great followers execute. And they also challenge, innovate, and expand the boundaries of what's possible. They provide the foundation for leadership because, simply put, leaders cannot lead without followers. Moreover, the most effective followers drive organizational impact. They align their contributions with broader goals, enabling teamwork, strategic alignment, and operational effectiveness.

How to Inspire Followership

David often shares an inspiring example about how to inspire followership. A company that includes a Followership Award in their recognition programs provides an incentive for positive effort. Along with awards for Leadership and Team Player, this company honors individuals who show strong followership. Nominees do not need to have formal leadership roles. They are recognized for guiding strategic processes, empowering others, and improving their team's effectiveness. Anyone could be nominated for one of the three categories:

1. **Best in Leadership:** "Guiding others to their fullest potential and empowering them to manifest a shared vision."

2. **Best Team Player:** "Going above and beyond to support peers and maximize the team's success."

3. **Best Follower:** "Exemplifying strategic partnership by actively contributing to the success of leadership and the broader mission."

This recognition shifts the narrative and centers the conversation around the qualities and value of good followership. Employees take pride in being excellent team players and contributors, knowing their role is just as vital as that of a formal leader. This system also validates those who thrive in individual contributor roles, making it acceptable—even admirable—not to seek leadership for its own sake.

Imagine the transformation this approach can bring. When you frame followership as a strategic partnership, it fosters collaboration, elevates team dynamics, and empowers individuals to make meaningful contributions. It builds a culture where leadership and followership aren't at odds but are two sides of the same coin, both essential for building resilient, high-performing teams.

What about your team? Do you create space for strategic followership and teamwork? If not, it might be time to pause and reflect: How can you elevate followership to drive both personal growth and organizational success? Here are a few key questions to consider:

How do you create space for strategic followership on your team?

Beyond recognizing leaders, do you also celebrate those who prioritize team goals and fully support the person in charge? How do you highlight and reward those individuals who set aside personal agendas to champion collective success? Recognizing followership as equally valuable to leadership sends a powerful message that both roles are essential for achieving shared goals.

How do you personally demonstrate followership?

Think about your role as a follower. How do you show up when someone else—a colleague, a peer, or one of your team members—takes the lead on a project or initiative? Are you fully engaged, offering thoughtful feedback, and supporting their efforts wholeheartedly? Or do you unintentionally hold back, waiting for your turn to enter the spotlight?

Great leaders are also exceptional team players. By demonstrating followership, you model the importance of setting personal ambitions aside to achieve a bigger goal. This could mean actively supporting a team member's leadership during a project, respecting their decision-making, or stepping in as a trusted partner to help them succeed. To gain loyalty, you need to give loyalty. Your actions as a follower set the tone for your team and reinforce that followership is a cornerstone of high performance.

How do you ensure your team members don't view followership as secondary to leadership?

When people see followership as a passive or subordinate role, it loses its value. Instead, you must elevate it to an active, strategic role that demands accountability, creativity, and collaboration. Creating a culture where followership is respected and celebrated ensures that your team understands its importance in driving results.

By setting the example of strategic followership, you send a clear message: Success requires that we put aside personal ambitions to serve a larger purpose. When leaders and followers embrace this mindset, and walk their talk, it creates a powerful ripple effect.

So the next time a team member takes the lead, offer them your support, align with their vision, and contribute to the team's collective success. In doing so, you strengthen your relationships and show your team that leadership and followership are equally vital, dynamic roles that contribute to long-term growth and impact.

At the end of the day, if you want to create a thriving team culture, your leadership is not enough. You must strive to be a great team member, demonstrate good followership, and encourage your team members to do the same. That means going beyond just doing your part—but actively supporting your leader and peers, fostering an inclusive environment, empowering autonomy, and building relationships beyond your immediate subgroup.

Here's what helped me and my clients to come together—and what I believe will help you as well:

1. Make sure both teams understand their purpose and how it contributes to the larger organizational mission.

2. Work on the Team Alignment Map to establish clarity on mutual expectations and work processes.

3. Coach team leaders to embrace a team-focused, followership approach—encouraging them to see the situation not just from their own team's perspective but also from the other team's point of view.

If you, as a leader, are facing challenges with another peer team, start by being a great follower for them. Find ways to support their purpose and agree on working together on a Team Alignment Map.

Great leaders don't lead in isolation. They rely on their teams just as much as their teams rely on them. So ask yourself: *How can I be a better team member?*

That's how you create a culture where everyone thrives when you show up for your team. And when the whole team thrives, the results will speak for themselves.

PART 3

INTEGRATED WORK

"Order and simplification are the first steps toward the mastery of a subject."

—Thomas Mann (1875–1955), German novelist and Nobel Prize laureate

The third pillar of the CLICK framework, Integrated Work, focuses on creating a clear, structured approach to daily collaboration. While the first two elements—Clear Purpose and Linking Connections—address broader dynamics like team vision and relationships, Integrated Work zeroes in on the operational mechanics that drive team success. It's about ensuring that the team's systems, processes, and norms are set up to empower collaboration and achieve goals efficiently.

Without a clear structure to guide work, even the most talented and motivated teams can fall prey to confusion, inefficiency, or conflict. That's why establishing shared guidelines for roles and responsibilities, communication protocols, and meeting practices—especially in hybrid or remote environments—is critical. These guidelines form a foundation for collaboration, offering teams structure and the flexibility to adapt.

When everyone knows what is expected of them—and what they can expect from each other—misunderstandings are minimized, friction is reduced, and focus remains on shared goals. Integrated Work ensures that team members aren't bogged down by operational inefficiencies, allowing them to channel their energy toward driving organizational growth.

Why does integrated work matter? When work is truly integrated, all team members' efforts and actions align, everyone is functioning as a cohesive unit toward a common goal. Operational aspects like workflows, communication, and decision-making processes all complement one another, whether in the office or across remote setups. This alignment is what transforms a group of individuals into a real CLICK team.

Why is this so important? Without integration, even the best intentions can result in inefficiencies, duplications, or gaps in responsibility. Imagine a research team in a cutting-edge lab, all working toward the same scientific breakthrough. A common goal unites them but the team lacks shared protocols for conducting experiments or recording results. Some duplicate efforts, others use conflicting methods, and critical discoveries are missed or misunderstood. Integrated Work is the process that brings everyone's contributions together. It helps turn individual efforts into a united and successful outcome. The same applies to business teams. Integrated Work ensures everyone pulls in the same direction, maximizing productivity while minimizing friction.

CHAPTER 7

STOP THE GUESSING: NAIL ROLES, EXPECTATIONS, AND OWNERSHIP

Unmet expectations—on both individual and team levels—are among the most significant sources of frustration in the workplace. Think about your work: how many times have you been annoyed because someone didn't follow through on what you expected? Or because you were blindsided by a request for something you didn't expect to be your responsibility? These scenarios often play out in the "shadow zones" where the boundaries of roles and responsibilities are unclear.

Here's what typically happens in these shadow zones:

- Loss of Clarity: Tasks or roles that were once clear begin to lose their sharp edges. What seemed straightforward yesterday becomes murky today.

- Drifting Accountability: Responsibilities start floating between team members. It often happens without explicit agreements or with no communication.

- Neglected Tasks: Work slips through the cracks because everyone assumes "someone else" is taking care of it.

- Duplicated Efforts: Multiple team members work on the same or similar task and are unaware of the overlap. And that leads to redundancy, inefficiency, and sometimes even conflict.

These frustrations are compounded by one key factor: No two people's roles are the same. Even if two employees hold the same title, their specific responsibilities might vary based on their skills, motivation, or how their manager interprets the role. This flexibility can be a strength, but it also introduces complexity when expectations aren't clearly defined or discussed.

Veiko Valkiainen, a leadership coach and researcher focused on self-managed organizations, shared something that really stuck with me: People often think they know their roles, but when you ask a few more questions, the edges start to blur. What exactly do they own? Where does their responsibility end? Where does someone else's begin?

It turns out that most teams carry around a lot of unspoken assumptions. Everything seems fine—until it isn't. Until something slips, or two people double up, or no one steps in at all.

High-performing teams don't wait for that moment. They take time—regularly—to make responsibilities visible and clear. This doesn't mean writing up a formal job description that never gets updated. It means being honest about how the work is evolving and making sure everyone stays on the same page.

(If you want to hear more of Veiko's insights on how role clarity supports autonomy and stronger collaboration, check out our full conversation on my YouTube channel.)

The challenge here is striking the right balance between overregulating roles and responsibilities and leaving them too open-ended. Overregulation—where every task is documented and controlled—might seem like a solution, but it quickly becomes outdated in fast-changing environments. You can't possibly foresee every task or scenario, and micromanagement creates rigidity that stifles creativity and ownership.

On the flip side, leaving roles and responsibilities entirely fluid is equally risky. I often see this trap in startups, where leaders pride themselves on being "agile" and resist defining clear boundaries because "everything is constantly changing." While agility is important, this lack of clarity can set employees—particularly new hires—up for failure. They're expected to "just know" their role, but without clear guidelines, they end up overwhelmed and uncertain.

What do we have as the result? We have frustrations pile up. Tasks linger in those shadow zones, creating friction and inefficiency. In self-sufficient teams, those shadow zones are addressed and minimized, but doing so requires intention. It's about having the conversations that others avoid—discussing expectations, clarifying boundaries, and making the gray areas visible so that tasks don't fall into the cracks.

The Hazards of Ambiguity: Jill's Story

When Jill joined the company as its new Digital Transformation Officer, she was excited. On paper, it seemed like the perfect next step in her career. With a proven track record leading digital transformation initiatives and a solid background as the CEO of a fast-growing software development company, she was confident she had what it took to succeed. She knew the market, understood the technology, and had built a career turning vision into reality.

The leadership team was equally enthusiastic. The CEO expressed his urgency for digital transformation and emphasized that Jill was exactly the person they needed to make it happen. "We need your input on how to execute it," he said. "And be sure to get input from all the stakeholders."

While these words seemed empowering at first, they concealed a red flag Jill overlooked: There were no clear expectations. Neither the CEO nor the leadership team had a unified vision of what digital transformation should achieve for the organization.

This lack of clarity became apparent almost immediately. Different stakeholders had different ideas of what Jill should prioritize, and none of them aligned. The marketing team wanted a new CRM system. The operations team pushed for automation in their processes. And the finance team? They were focused on better analytics dashboards.

Jill found herself in a reactive mode, fixing automations for various departments. She knew these weren't the transformational initiatives she was hired to lead, but she figured they were "quick wins" that could build goodwill and pave the way for broader changes. Unfortunately, it didn't work. The stakeholders, dissatisfied with their unmet and varied expectations, started voicing frustration. The CEO, who deferred to his team without offering much direct guidance, decided Jill wasn't the right fit for the role.

And just like that, what could have been a promising career move ended in disappointment—for Jill and the company.

Lessons from Jill's Story

Jill's experience highlights a common pitfall when organizations onboard new team members: a lack of clarity around roles, responsibilities, and expectations. This isn't just a problem for the new hire. It's a systemic issue that impacts the entire team.

Let's break down where things went wrong:

1. **Unclear Role Definition:**

Jill's position was created during the digital transformation "hype" period. Everyone thought they needed a Digital Transformation Officer, but no one in the organization understood *why* or *what for*. Without a clear purpose or agreed-upon outcomes for the role, Jill was set up for failure from day one.

2. **Mismatched Expectations:**

Stakeholders had different, often conflicting, ideas about what Jill should accomplish. In the absence of a shared vision, each department treated her as a resource to fix their immediate problems rather than as a leader driving long-term strategic change.

3. **Missed Opportunities for Alignment:**

While Jill could have clarified expectations during the interview process or in her early days on the job, she didn't. This oversight meant she entered the role without a firm understanding of what success looked like in the organization's eyes.

The Role of Clarity in Onboarding

Jill's story isn't unique. When a new person joins a team, it's not just about filling a vacancy—it's about creating alignment. Every team member must have clarity on:

- **The Role's Purpose:** Why does this position exist? How does it contribute to the broader organizational goals?

- **Key Responsibilities:** What specific tasks and areas fall under this person's purview? Just as importantly, what doesn't?

- **Expected Outcomes:** What does success look like in six months? A year?

Without addressing these elements, new hires are left to navigate shadow zones, where responsibilities are undefined, accountability is ambiguous, and frustrations run high.

How to Avoid Jill's Fate

Whether you're the new hire stepping into a role or the leader welcoming someone to the team, it's critical to establish clarity from the outset. Here's how:

1. Ask the Right Questions During the Hiring Process:

As a candidate, it's essential to go beyond generic role descriptions. Ask specific questions like:

- What does success look like for this role in the first six months?
- How does this role interact with other departments?

- Are there any existing challenges or tensions I should be aware of?

Leaders should also proactively outline these expectations during interviews to ensure alignment.

2. Prioritize an Alignment Session Early On:

Within the first week, schedule a meeting with the key stakeholders for the role. Use this time to:

- Agree on the top priorities for the role.
- Discuss how success will be measured.
- Address any grey areas in responsibilities.

3. Create a Living Job Description:

Roles in dynamic environments evolve. Document the core responsibilities and update them regularly based on organizational needs. This ensures both the new hire and the team have a clear understanding of what's expected. Make sure the document is known to the person in this role, their manager, team members and key stakeholders.

4. Encourage Open Communication:

Leaders should check in regularly, not just on performance but on role clarity. Questions like "What do you need from me to succeed?" or "Are there any responsibilities you're unclear about?" can make a big difference.

When onboarding is done right, it sets the foundation for success—not just for the new hire but for the entire team. Clarity transforms shadow zones into defined boundaries, where expectations are met, responsibilities are shared, and collaboration thrives.

If Jill's story resonates with you—whether as the new hire or the leader—it's not too late to course-correct. Clarity isn't something you establish once and forget; it's an ongoing process that keeps your team aligned and thriving.

Creating Clarity with The Team Clarity Compass

So how can you, as a team, bring clarity to roles and responsibilities? One effective way is to use **The Team Clarity Compass**—a structured exercise designed to align roles, responsibilities, and expectations through a combination of reflection and team discussion. This brings clarity and fosters accountability and trust among team members.

Here's how it works:

The Team Clarity Compass exercise

Objective:

To help teams align on roles, responsibilities, and mutual expectations through structured reflection and discussion.

Why The Team Clarity Compass Works:

- **Encourages Transparency:** It provides a safe and structured platform for open dialogue, ensuring everyone is on the same page.
- **Reduces Misunderstandings:** By surfacing and addressing mismatched expectations, the team can minimize future frustrations and conflicts.
- **Improves Accountability:** Each participant leaves with a personal commitment document that clearly defines their role and responsibilities.
- **Flexible for Any Team:** Works equally well for remote, hybrid, or in-person teams. Great of C-Suite, product, project or functional teams.

This exercise builds effectively on previous team discussions. If your team has already clarified its Purpose Statement, explored shared values (including 'Keep It Up' and 'Cut It Out' behaviors), and mapped key stakeholders, members will likely find it easier to articulate their roles and expectations. Having that foundation helps ensure contributions are aligned with the team's broader direction and agreed-upon norms.

Preparation

1. Prepare the Templates[11]:

- **Define Template Sections:** Ensure your chosen template (whether digital or physical) includes distinct sections for each participant to complete. These sections should cover:

  - Role Description: What is your primary role within the team?

  - Key Contributions: How do you add value to the team?

  - Responsibilities: What specific tasks or areas are you accountable for?

  - Expected Outcomes: What measurable results are you expected to achieve?

  - Expectations of Others: What do you need from teammates to succeed?

2. Set Up the Workspace:

For in-person sessions: Arrange the room for open collaboration. Provide printed templates, pens, markers, and a whiteboard or flip chart.

For online sessions: Share digital templates through collaborative tools like Google Docs or Miro. Use video conferencing tools with breakout room functionality for discussions.

3. Communicate the Objectives:

---

[11] Note: You can find downloadable template examples on my website dariarudnik.com.

Send a brief to participants before the session, outlining the purpose of the activity, its structure, and what they need to prepare.

How to Conduct the Team Clarity Compass Workshop

Step 1: Individual Reflection (10–15 minutes)

Ask participants to independently fill out their templates, focusing on:

- Their understanding of their own role.
- Key contributions they bring to the team.
- Specific responsibilities they handle.
- The measurable outcomes they are striving to achieve.

Encourage them to be as specific and detailed as possible.

Step 2: Aligning Expectations (10 minutes)

Each participant completes the "Expectations of Others" section, detailing:

- What they rely on their colleagues for.
- Key actions, information, or outcomes they need from others to succeed in their role.

Step 3: Reviewing Expectations (15 minutes)

- Participants now review the expectations others have documented for them.

    - **In Person:** Physically exchange the completed forms.
    - **Online:** Share document links, duplicate relevant sections into a shared space, or use collaboration tool features to allow participants to view the 'Expectations of Others' sections that apply to them.

- As they review, participants should:

  - Mark expectations they understand and agree with using a ✓.
  - Mark expectations they disagree with or find unclear using an X.

- This simple marking step surfaces potential misalignments and discussion points for the next step.

Step 4: Collaborative Discussion (30–45 minutes)

Bring the team together to discuss the expectations marked with X. The goal is to:

- Resolve disagreements about responsibilities.
- Clarify ambiguous tasks.
- Reassign responsibilities if necessary.

This step requires open and constructive communication. As the facilitator of this discussion, ensure that the conversation remains focused and respectful. Use visual aids like a whiteboard (offline) or shared screens (online) to track progress and highlight unresolved points.

Step 5: Finalizing Commitments (15 minutes)

Once everyone agrees on roles and expectations, update your forms to reflect the final decisions. These documents act as personal commitments to ensure accountability moving forward.

If any unresolved issues remain, schedule a follow-up meeting with the necessary participants and set a deadline to finalize the document.

Wrap-Up and Follow-Up

1. Recap Key Agreements:

Summarize what was decided and stress the importance of clear communication to keep the team aligned.

2. Encourage Accountability:

Remind team members to review their commitments regularly, especially during performance reviews or project planning.

3. Make Clarity a Habit:

Integrate The Team Clarity Compass into your team's workflow, using it at key moments like onboarding new members or launching new projects.

The Team Clarity Compass is a valuable tool for improving teamwork and communication. By fostering open discussions about roles and expectations, it helps teams:

- Avoid misunderstandings before they become bigger issues.
- Improve collaboration by clarifying how team members rely on each other.
- Build trust and accountability, ensuring everyone understands their role and impact.

Teams that prioritize clarity tend to perform better. Take Jill's experience, for example—when her company didn't clearly define her responsibilities as a Digital Transformation Officer, it led to confusion, frustration, and missed opportunities. If leadership had used The Team Clarity Compass during her onboarding, they could have aligned expectations from the start, preventing role ambiguity and setting her up for success.

Making The Team Clarity Compass a regular part of your team's workflow ensures that no one is left wondering about their role or value. Instead, every team member has a clear roadmap, leading to better performance and stronger team dynamics.

Turning Chaos into Clarity: A Startup Accelerator's Transformation

Clarity doesn't just prevent frustration; it can save relationships, reputations, and revenue. A leadership team at a startup accelerator nearly lost a major client due to severe communication breakdowns.

Their client, one of their most prominent partners, had become deeply frustrated. They were being asked the same questions multiple times by different team members, and important information they requested seemed to vanish into thin air. No one followed up. No one took ownership. What should have been a smooth, professional experience turned into a chaotic and uncoordinated mess.

Tensions flared within the team. Marketing blamed sales for not closing the loop. Sales pointed fingers at the product team for not providing the right information. Everyone piled on quality assurance, accusing them of slowing things down and adding extra work. Stress levels were at an all-time high, and the founders—who were already juggling multiple businesses—felt completely overwhelmed.

When the founders brought me in to assess the situation, one issue immediately stood out: There was no clarity in roles or responsibilities. Expectations were vague, overlapping, or simply ignored. Who was responsible for the number of startups joining the programs—sales or marketing? Who owned participant satisfaction? Who was in charge of ensuring participants actually attended the events? These unanswered questions left critical tasks lingering in the shadow zone, with no one stepping up to claim them.

How The Team Clarity Compass Helped Save the Day

We began with The Team Clarity Compass, but it was clear from the start that this wouldn't be a quick fix. The team had deep-seated issues that needed unraveling. Over three two-hour sessions, we worked through the mess together.

Session 1: Identifying Agreed-Upon Responsibilities

We started by listing responsibilities that everyone could unanimously agree belonged to specific roles. This step helped create an initial framework, but it also surfaced a glaring issue: There was a *long* list of unclaimed or contested tasks.

Session 2: Tackling the Shadow Zone

Next, we focused on the tasks that had fallen into the cracks. Some were responsibilities claimed by multiple team members, causing duplication and inefficiency. Others were tasks that no one wanted, leaving critical work undone. These discussions were not easy—they brought underlying tensions to the surface—but they were necessary to untangle the confusion.

Session 3: Finalizing Commitments and Realigning the Team

By the end of the third session, every team member had a clear, documented list of responsibilities and commitments. No more guesswork. No more blaming. Just accountability.

But the team didn't stop there. Through these discussions, they identified a much larger issue: The founders were acting as de facto managers. Every problem, question, and escalation was landing on their plates. As a result, the founders were stretched thin, and the team lacked cohesive leadership.

And the team had a solution. They proposed appointing a CEO—a dedicated leader to act as their representative to the founders. This person—one of the current team members—would not only handle communication with the founders but also take ownership of aligning the C-Suite team and ensuring accountability across functions.

This new structure, combined with the clarity they achieved through The Team Clarity Compass, made all the difference.

- **Roles and Responsibilities:** Each team member knew exactly what they were accountable for, eliminating overlap and gaps.

- **Improved Client Relationship:** With clear ownership, the team resolved the client's concerns and even secured an extension for another accelerator program.

- **Streamlined Communication:** The CEO became the central point of contact, reducing the noise and allowing the founders to focus on their broader responsibilities.

When Clarity Creates Opportunity

What happened at the startup accelerator isn't unique—it's a pattern repeated across organizations of all sizes. Misaligned expectations, unclear roles, and tasks slipping through the cracks can disrupt even the most skilled teams. But with clarity, everything changes.

By using The Team Clarity Compass, the accelerator team was able to do more than solve their immediate challenges. They built stronger relationships with their clients, improved the way they worked together, and created a system that could grow with them.

This shows how powerful clarity can be. When people understand their roles, know what's expected, and take ownership, things start to flow. The confusion disappears, work gets done, and teams feel more connected.

If you've ever been in a situation where responsibilities felt unclear or things kept falling through the cracks, you're not alone. Tools like The Team Clarity Compass can help bring everything into focus. It takes effort, but the results—better teamwork, trust, and performance—are absolutely worth it.

CHAPTER 8

DESIGN MEETINGS THAT DRIVE PROGRESS

Back-to-back meetings from 9 a.m. to 6 p.m., with barely enough time to grab a coffee, let alone focus on deep work, as if the calendar controls you instead of the other way around. Every conversation feels like a repeat of the last, decisions postponed to yet another meeting, and the to-do list grows longer by the end of the day. And the real work was delayed for hours, or even days, until these meetings ended… Sound familiar?

If you've ever ended a long day wondering how you were in meetings for 10 hours but still made no real progress, you're not alone. Research[12] consistently shows that meetings consume more of our time than ever before—yet their effectiveness remains questionable.

- Employees spend 25 to 30% of their time in meetings.
- Meetings consume 72% of executives' time—often leaving them little space for strategic thinking.

---

[12] Stop the Meeting Madness https://hbr.org/2017/07/stop-the-meeting-madness

- According to McKinsey[13], 61% of executives say at least half of the time spent making decisions in meetings is ineffective.

Meetings aren't inherently bad. When done right, they drive alignment, spark innovation, and help teams move forward. But let's be honest: Most meetings don't do that. Instead, they derail productivity, drain energy, and leave people scrambling to catch up on their actual work.

So why do we keep scheduling them? Because it feels like the only way to get things done. We assume that bringing everyone into a room (or onto a Zoom call) is the best way to collaborate. But when meetings become the default—rather than a strategic tool—they quickly become a waste of time.

This chapter is about breaking that cycle. Your team doesn't need more meetings; you need better meetings—and fewer of them. And you can do it if you rethink when and why you need to meet in the first place.

By the end of this chapter, you'll have a simple, actionable framework to help you:

- Cut down unnecessary meetings without losing alignment.
- Make meetings more productive and engaging.
- Free up more time for deep, focused work.

Because the goal isn't just to have fewer meetings—it's to have better meetings that actually move work forward. Let's dive in.

Communication Matrix

Not every conversation needs a meeting. But somewhere along the way, meetings became the default way to communicate—whether it's sharing updates, asking a quick question, or brainstorming ideas. As a result of it, we now have overloaded calendars, fragmented focus, and frustration.

---

[13] What is an effective meeting? https://www.mckinsey.com/featured-insights/mckinsey-explainers/what-is-an-effective-meeting

When the day is packed with meetings, people are forced to do their actual work early in the morning, late at night, or in between calls.

Some might say ditch the meetings, but in reality, meetings are not the problem, how we use them is. Instead of treating them as a catch-all for every discussion, decision, or update, we need to decide when a meeting is necessary and when it's not. How do you do that? I teach the teams and leaders I coach to use Communication Matrix.

Communication Matrix helps teams make better decisions about choosing the best communication channel by asking two key questions:

1. Concise vs. Comprehensive – Is the message short and to the point, or does it require an in-depth discussion with multiple perspectives?

2. Synchronous vs. Asynchronous – Does this conversation need to happen in real time, or can people respond at their convenience?

You can instantly determine the best communication method by answering these two questions instead of defaulting to a meeting.

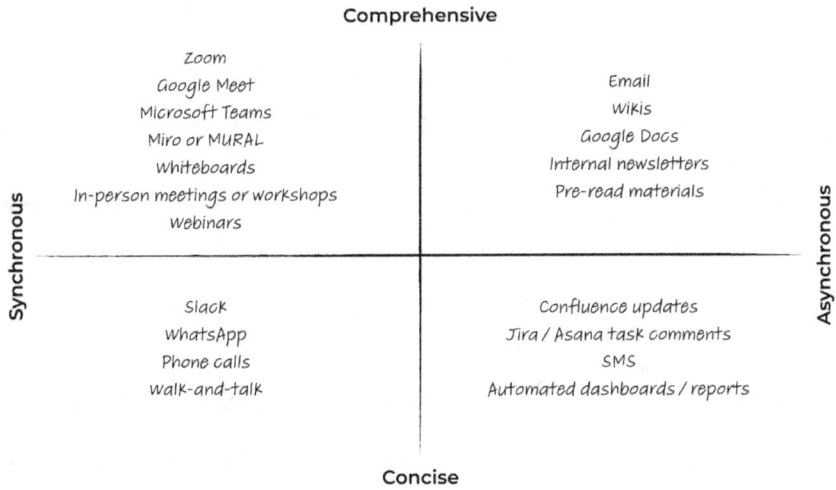

How the Communication Matrix Works:

Concise Synchronous – Quick, Real-Time Interactions

Use this for fast, to-the-point conversations that require an immediate response. Think of it as a quick huddle rather than a formal meeting.

Examples:

- Slack messages or quick DMs for urgent clarifications
- A short phone call to resolve a time-sensitive issue
- A brief check-in when an answer is needed right away

This type of communication is best for solving small roadblocks quickly without waiting for a full meeting.

Comprehensive Synchronous – Deep-Dive, Real-Time Discussions

Some conversations truly require face-to-face (or virtual) interaction. These are the meetings that should exist—ones where real-time collaboration is valuable.

Examples:

- Strategy sessions that need brainstorming and live discussion
- Decision-making meetings where back-and-forth conversation is required
- Crisis response discussions where immediate alignment is critical

For these meetings, preparation is key—participants should come ready with the necessary information to use time efficiently.

Concise Asynchronous – Simple, One-Way Communication

If you're sharing an update or asking a question that doesn't need an immediate reply, it's better to handle it asynchronously.

Examples:

- Quick emails or messages with status updates
- A note in a shared document instead of scheduling a meeting
- A project check-in via collaboration tools like Notion or Asana

This keeps communication efficient and unobtrusive so people can respond when it fits into their workflow.

Comprehensive Asynchronous – Detailed, Thoughtful Communication

Some discussions require depth and context, but not a meeting. These are best suited for asynchronous formats that allow people to review and respond thoughtfully.

Examples:

- Detailed reports or project proposals that need review
- Recorded video messages explaining complex topics
- Written strategic plans that team members can digest on their own time

This type of communication ensures that people have time to process information and contribute meaningfully rather than reacting on the spot in a meeting.

The Golden Rule: If you can do it asynchronously, that's how it should be.

The most productive teams aren't the ones that meet the most— they're the ones that communicate effectively. By choosing the right method for each type of conversation, you can cut down on unnecessary meetings while keeping everyone aligned and informed.

Choose the Meeting Energy

The Communication Matrix helps reduce unnecessary meetings by shifting conversations to the right format. However, even when a meeting is necessary, not all meetings should be treated the same way. While the Communication Matrix helps you decide if a synchronous meeting is needed and what channel to use, we also need to consider the purpose and energy of the meetings we do hold. A brainstorming session shouldn't run like a project execution meeting, and a strategic planning discussion requires different energy than an alignment on crisis communication.

One of the biggest reasons meetings feel unproductive is that they lack clarity of purpose. People walk in unsure why they're there, what's expected of them, or what the meeting should accomplish. That is the main reason for discussions to go in circles, people to disengage, and decisions to get postponed to—yet another meeting.

The best way to treat this vicious cycle is to define the type of meeting when you plan it.

Step 1: Identify the Meeting Type – Do You Even Need One?

Before scheduling any meeting, ask yourself: What is the real goal?

1. If the goal is decision-making, brainstorming, execution, or alignment, a meeting makes sense.

- These require real-time discussion, collaboration, and input from multiple people.

2. If the goal is to share updates or information, skip the meeting.

- Use email, project management tools, or recorded videos instead.

Still unsure? Consider this:

- Are you expecting participants to contribute ideas, perspectives, or decisions? → Yes? You need a meeting.

- Will people mostly be listening and receiving information? →
  Yes? Then, you better handle it asynchronously.

Too often, meetings are called simply because it seems like the "right" thing to do. But the best teams challenge this assumption and only meet when it's truly necessary.

If a meeting is required, the next step is ensuring it's structured correctly based on the type of conversation it involves.

Step 2: Match the Meeting to the Energy It Requires

Every meeting benefits from a specific type of energy and focus. To understand these varying contributions, we can draw on The GC Index® framework. The GC Index® is regarded as the world's first organimetric[14], a tool designed to measure how individuals and teams naturally direct their energy to make an impact. It identifies five key ways people contribute: Game Changer (radical ideas), Strategist (planning), Play Maker (team cohesion), Implementer (delivery), and Polisher (refinement). Matching your meeting type to the dominant energy required helps ensure purposeful collaboration.

---

[14] The GC Index is recognised as an Organimetric by the International Test Commission (ITC). The GC Index in its creation and development adheres to the ITC guidelines, which are internationally accepted as the gold standard in testing and assessment regardless of jurisdiction

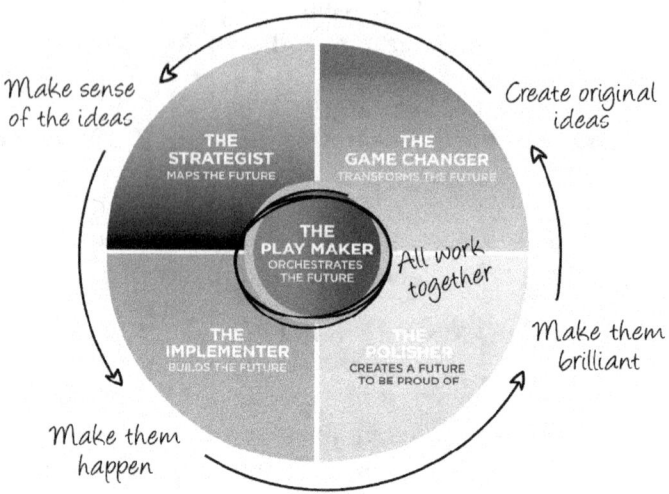

Consider these GC Index types:

Game Changer Brainstorm Session – When the goal is invention, innovation, and breakthrough ideas.

- Best for exploring new possibilities, solving big challenges, and thinking beyond the status quo.
- Example: A marketing team brainstorming a new campaign or a product team reimagining a key feature.

Best Practices:

- Create a judgment-free space for open discussion.
- Encourage wild ideas without immediately shooting them down.
- Use tools like mind mapping, sticky notes, or visual brainstorming boards.

Strategist Visioning Workshop – When the goal is long-term planning and strategic alignment.

- Best for defining the organization's future direction, making high-level decisions, or setting priorities.
- Example: A leadership team mapping out the next five-year growth strategy.

Best Practices:

- Provide pre-read materials so everyone is informed beforehand.
- Use structured planning frameworks to guide discussion.
- Allow time for critical analysis and debate before making decisions.

Play Maker Collaborative Alignment Meeting – When the goal is getting teams on the same page.

- Best for aligning different teams, clarifying expectations, and ensuring smooth collaboration.
- Example: A cross-functional meeting between sales, marketing, and product teams to ensure a product launch runs smoothly.

Best Practices:

- Define clear objectives before the meeting.
- Encourage open communication between departments.
- Establish a follow-up plan with assigned responsibilities.

Implementer Execution-Focused Roundtable – When the goal is turning strategy into action.

- Best for breaking big goals into smaller tasks, assigning ownership, and setting deadlines.
- Example: A project kick-off meeting where specific deliverables and timelines are assigned.

Best Practices:

- Have a structured agenda to ensure clarity.

- Focus on assigning action items rather than open-ended discussions.

- Use task management tools to track progress.

Polisher Quality Review – When the goal is improving existing work and refining details.

- Best for reviewing performance, ensuring quality, and making continuous improvements.

- Example: A team reviewing customer feedback to refine an existing product or service.

Best Practices:

- Use review checklists to assess progress.

- Foster a constructive feedback culture.

- Track improvements over time and adjust processes as needed.

Selecting the right type of meeting improves focus, engagement, and efficiency—ensuring that discussions lead to tangible outcomes.

Meetings should never feel like a waste of time—but they will if you don't structure them with a clear purpose. By identifying the right type of meeting and matching it to the energy required, you create an environment where meetings are not just necessary—but productive and valuable.

Set Meeting Norms

Even when you have the correct type of meeting, it can still go off the rails if there aren't explicit norms. Too many meetings lack structure—people show up unprepared, discussions wander, and no real decisions have been made by the end. To prevent this, your team needs a set of meeting norms that ensure every meeting is efficient, purposeful, and action-driven.

If I could choose only one thing to change in how teams work that will have the maximum impact on teams' performance and well-being,

I'd say—implement the Meeting Norms. These four essential norms will immediately improve the quality of your meetings:

1. No Agenda, No Meeting – It's Non-Negotiable

Meetings without a detailed agenda waste time and frustrate participants. A well-structured agenda sets expectations, keeps discussions focused, and ensures productive meetings.

Best Practices:

- Every meeting must have an agenda shared in advance. If there's no agenda, the meeting should be canceled or declined.
- Agendas should outline key discussion points, objectives, and expected outcomes to keep everyone on track.
- Encourage participants to review the agenda beforehand so they come prepared.

If you can't think of valuable objectives or clear outcomes, then maybe this shouldn't be a meeting, and you can use another communication method.

2. Respect Time – Cap Meetings at 45 Minutes

Most discussions don't need an hour. If you have a clear agenda, you'll have a structured conversation and develop the action plan earlier. However, if you schedule it for a full 60 minutes—you'll sit through all of the scheduled time.

Best Practices:

- Cap meetings at 45 minutes. If you need longer, break it into focused segments or follow-ups.
- If you have a more extended workshop or strategy session, include technical breaks for people to stretch.
- Start and end on time. Don't wait for latecomers—respect the time of those who arrive as scheduled.

When you have 45 minutes instead of one hour or 25 minutes instead of 30, you stop having back-to-back meetings and give people time to recharge and prepare for their next activity.

3. Assign Clear Roles to Keep the Meeting on Track

Without structure, meetings can become chaotic. Assigning specific roles helps keep discussions focused, documented, and efficient.

Essential Meeting Roles:

- Facilitator – Guides the discussion, ensures the agenda is followed, and keeps the conversation productive.
- Note-Taker – Captures key decisions, action items, and next steps and summarizes these after the meeting.
- Time-Keeper – Ensures the meeting stays on schedule, nudging the group to move on when necessary.

One person can handle multiple roles. During regular team meetings, you can switch roles, share them between different team members, and have everyone actively involved.

4. No Meeting Ends Without Decisions and Next Steps

Too many meetings end without clear outcomes, requiring another meeting to continue the discussion.

Best Practices:

- Every meeting should end with clear action items—who is doing what, by when?
- Document all decisions so there's a shared understanding of the next steps.
- Circulate a quick summary afterward so everyone is aligned.

A great meeting doesn't just end—it moves work forward; otherwise, you've wasted time there.

Some people resist meeting norms because they fear making meetings too rigid. And it takes time to get used to the new structure. But when you make meetings work for you, you'll ensure that time spent in meetings is productive, and people can spend the rest of their time on meaningful tasks.

By setting these norms, you'll see immediate improvements in engagement, decision-making, and overall team efficiency.

How a Retail Leader Took Back His Time

James stepped into his role as a new store manager six months ago at a well-known retail chain. His flagship location was once a top revenue generator for the company, but things had been sliding. Sales stagnated, operations became inefficient, and his team seemed to lack initiative, constantly looking to him for decisions.

He wanted to turn things around. But there was a problem. He had no time to think.

His calendar was packed from morning to evening. Daily check-ins with store managers, one-on-ones, leadership meetings, and team huddles never ended. By the time he wrapped up his last meeting, he had no energy for big-picture planning. Instead of working on fixing the store's performance, he was caught in a cycle of talking about the same problems over and over again.

James realized something had to change. He needed to control his time and help his team become more independent if he wanted better results. Here's what he did:

1. **Protecting Time for Thinking and Strategy**

The first step was simple: blocking time on his calendar for deep work.

He set aside dedicated weekly hours—no meetings, no interruptions—just time to focus on financial reports, store layout improvements, and long-term strategy. This gave him the space to analyze what was working, what wasn't, and what needed to change instead of constantly reacting to problems.

2. Turning Daily Meetings into Asynchronous Updates

James looked at his schedule and asked, "Do we really need to have all these meetings?"

The answer was no. James stopped gathering his store managers every morning for an update. Instead, he asked each store manager to send a structured email covering key numbers, staffing, and operational concerns to the whole team.

Instead of spending an hour in a meeting, James and his team could read the updates on their own time and focus meetings on actual decision-making.

3. Letting the Team Run Their Meetings

James had always led the weekly team meetings, but then he decided to try something different. He knew that his team was relying on him too much. If there were a problem, they'd wait for a meeting to discuss it rather than solve it alone.

So he rotated the leadership of team meetings. A different team member ran the discussion each week—setting the agenda, facilitating the conversation, and guiding problem-solving.

At first, people accepted this with caution. But then, slowly, they started stepping up. They stopped waiting for the meeting to solve a problem and began taking ownership of issues instead of always looking to him for answers.

4. Enforcing a "No Agenda, No Meeting" Rule

James made a firm decision: Without a clear agenda, the meeting wouldn't happen.

Meetings used to start with vague discussions, drift into unrelated topics, and end with no clear decisions. Now, every meeting had a clear purpose, discussion points, and expected outcomes. If someone didn't prepare an agenda, James declined the meeting.

It didn't necessarily result in fewer meetings, but they definitely became more focused and productive.

At first, some employees were unsure about the changes. They were used to bringing every minor issue to a meeting. But over time, James noticed a shift:

The team became more self-sufficient. Instead of waiting for meetings, they started solving problems themselves.

Collaboration improved. Team members talked to each other more instead of always running to the manager.

A long-term strategy was created—and acted on. With time to think, James and his team mapped out a clear plan for the year and got approval from the company's leadership.

The store's financial performance improved. With more time spent on strategy and execution, the store climbed back up the rankings.

Meetings should be a tool to move work forward—not something that keeps you from doing real work. If you're constantly stuck in discussions, where is the time to actually improve performance?

This chapter has given you strategies to take back control of your time, make meetings more meaningful, and create a more independent team.

CHAPTER 9

MASTERING REMOTE AND HYBRID COLLABORATION

I remember sitting through a virtual meeting, watching faces flicker on the screen, and thinking, *There has to be a better way to collaborate remotely.* I'm sure you've been there.

Remote and hybrid teams are now the norm, yet many still struggle to work together effectively. Despite all the tools available—video calls, instant messaging, shared documents—something often feels off. The energy, the clarity, the natural flow of collaboration just isn't the same.

When I started analyzing this, I noticed that many teams assume they can simply take what worked in an office and move it online without adjusting how they operate. But remote and hybrid work require a different approach. The biggest mistake companies make is trying to copy-paste in-office collaboration into a virtual setting. Meetings that worked in person can feel slow and frustrating online. Important updates that once spread naturally—through quick desk chats or hallway conversations—now get lost. And those spontaneous moments where ideas sparked? They don't happen unless they're deliberately created.

To make remote and hybrid teams truly effective, we have to rethink how we collaborate. That means reworking brainstorming sessions, restructuring communication, and intentionally creating opportunities for connection.

This chapter will show you how to make those shifts so your team thrives in remote settings, feels connected, and becomes part of an amazing team that truly clicks.

Why Traditional Collaboration Fails in Remote/Hybrid Setups

In a physical office, communication happens naturally. You overhear conversations, get quick clarifications over coffee, and run into colleagues between meetings. Even if you miss an official announcement, someone will likely mention it in passing. These informal touch points help keep everyone aligned without much effort.

In a remote setting, if something isn't explicitly shared, it doesn't exist. There are no chance encounters or side conversations to fill in gaps. If updates aren't intentionally documented and repeated across multiple channels, people miss them—leading to misalignment, confusion, and delays.

Then there's the challenge of relationships. In an office, even if you don't work directly with someone, you still get to know them. You might chat while grabbing lunch, exchange small talk before a meeting, or collaborate on a cross-team project. These casual interactions build trust and make future collaboration easier.

Remote teams don't have that luxury. Without deliberate effort, people become isolated, interacting only with their immediate team. Cross-team relationships don't form naturally, making it harder to collaborate when needed.

Remote and hybrid teams don't struggle because they lack tools. In fact, they have a lot and sometimes too many tools to manage. The real reason they struggle is that they haven't adapted their ways of working. Communication, brainstorming, and relationship-building all require a different approach in a virtual environment.

One of the biggest challenges is virtual collaboration. I'm sure you've all seen it—team meetings where energy fades, participation drops, and only a few voices dominate the conversation. Virtual collaboration often suffers from:

- **Production blocking** – Since only one person can speak at a time, others hold back their thoughts, sometimes losing them entirely.

- **Evaluation apprehension** – People worry about being judged, making them less likely to share bold or unconventional ideas.

- **Groupthink** – The need for harmony leads teams to settle for "safe" ideas instead of pushing boundaries.

- **Social loafing** – In larger virtual meetings, some people disengage, assuming others will contribute instead.

To make remote collaboration work, teams need new methods that fit the realities of virtual work. And let's start by improving communication and building stronger connections—so that distance doesn't get in the way of working effectively.

Fixing Communication in Remote and Hybrid Teams

Remote work demands intentional communication. It means that teams need to structure their communication so that the right information reaches the right people at the right time.

Key Principles of Remote Communication

Over-communicate intentionally – Important information needs to be stated clearly and reinforced. In a remote setting, repetition isn't annoying—it's necessary. If something is critical, share it in multiple places to ensure it gets seen.

Use multiple channels for key updates – In an office, a single announcement in a meeting might be enough. Remotely, you need to follow up in writing. Major decisions should be shared in email, chat, and documented in a central place like a shared doc or project management tool.

Replace casual in-office conversations with structured updates – Instead of relying on impromptu discussions, set up **asynchronous check-ins** where people can share progress, ask questions, and stay aligned—without needing another meeting.

Types of Communication and How to Adapt to Them

Not all communication works the same way in a remote or hybrid team. The key is **recognizing what's missing** and being intentional about how you replace it.

Information Sharing

- **In an office:** You pick up updates naturally—by overhearing conversations, chatting before meetings, or catching an announcement in person.
- **Remotely:** Updates must be explicit and repeated across multiple channels. One announcement isn't enough—people need reminders in different formats (email, chat, project tools).

Decision-Making

- **In an office:** A quick hallway chat or impromptu meeting can resolve a decision on the spot.
- **Remotely:** Every decision needs clear documentation—who decided what, why, and what happens next. Without it, people miss context or question what was agreed upon.

Relationship-Building

- **In an office:** You naturally get to know coworkers over lunch, in meetings, or just by being around them.

- **Remotely:** You need structured opportunities for connection. This could be virtual coffee chats, cross-team introductions, or intentional networking to ensure people build relationships beyond their immediate teams.

Better Calls, Better Team

A Learning & Development (L&D) team at an engineering consulting firm had a pretty big job on their hands. They were responsible for all the training and development programs for 5,000 employees spread across multiple locations. Some team members had been around for years, while others were new and had never even met their coworkers in person. Everything they did was remote—meetings, collaboration, you name it.

On the surface, everything appeared to function smoothly. However, beneath that surface, there were subtle cracks. Newer team members often remained quiet during meetings, hesitant to voice their thoughts or contribute ideas. This silence wasn't due to a lack of interest or capability but rather a sense of disconnect and uncertainty about how to navigate the remote work environment.

The team's manager, Derek, recognized this issue. He understood that for the team to thrive, everyone needed to feel comfortable communicating and aligned on how they worked together. But fostering that sense of connection in a remote setting wasn't easy. To address this, Derek brought in a consultant—me—to help the team reevaluate and improve their communication practices.

We began by holding several team sessions focused on communication. These weren't generic discussions about "improving collaboration" but rather deep dives into the specifics of how the team interacted. We analyzed the various channels they used—or didn't use—and categorized them into the Communication Matrix: concise synchronous (quick real-time exchanges), comprehensive synchronous (detailed real-time discussions), concise asynchronous (brief non-real-time updates), and comprehensive asynchronous (detailed non-real-time information sharing). This structured approach helped the team see where gaps existed and where improvements could be made.

One of the ideas that emerged was the use of phone calls as a communication tool. Not video calls or conference calls, but traditional voice-only phone calls. Some team members suggested that phone calls could be an efficient way to handle quick check-ins, ask brief questions, or provide immediate feedback without the formality of scheduling a meeting. At first, this seemed like a practical solution. However, during one of the sessions, a team member, Kate, shared something that we did not expect.

Kate admitted that whenever her manager called her, she felt a surge of anxiety. Her immediate assumption was that something was wrong—an emergency, a mistake, or some urgent issue that required her attention. This reaction wasn't based on anything her manager had done intentionally; it was simply a subconscious response to the unexpected nature of the call. As Kate spoke, a few other team members nodded in agreement, revealing that they, too, felt uneasy about receiving unscheduled phone calls.

Derek was surprised by this revelation. He had never considered that his calls might be causing stress. "I had no idea you felt that way," he said. "I thought it was just a quick and easy way to connect." This moment of honesty led to a constructive discussion about how to make phone calls less intimidating. The team agreed that before making a call, the caller would send a brief message to give the recipient context. For example: *"Hi, I'm going to call you in a few minutes to discuss X. Nothing urgent—just a quick check-in."* This small adjustment helped alleviate the anxiety some team members felt and made phone calls a more effective communication tool.

Over time, this change, combined with other improvements in how the team structured their communication, had a significant impact. They began using the right channels for the right types of information. Quick updates were shared via messaging platforms. Decisions made during meetings were documented in emails and stored in a shared drive for easy reference. Phone calls, now preceded by a quick message, became a useful way to handle brief, real-time exchanges.

The results were transformative. Team members who had previously been quiet began to speak up, sharing ideas and contributing to discussions. The team felt more connected, more aligned, and more productive. This shift in communication dynamics enabled them to design and deliver exceptional learning and development programs for the organization. By ensuring that everyone felt heard and included, they created an environment where collaboration thrived.

Effective communication in a remote work environment is never about the tools. You can use anything you like as long as you have your team's communication strategy and structure. By paying attention to the nuances of how people interact and making thoughtful adjustments, even small changes can lead to significant improvements. And for this team, the journey to better communication was not so much about efficiency— they were ok even before we started working together. What they've gained is trust, inclusion, and a space where everyone could contribute their best. And that led to better engagement and long-term productivity.

If the situation in Derek's team looks familiar, one of your most important jobs is to create intentional connection points for your remote team members to build connection and trust. These are the virtual equivalent of lunchroom conversations and office banter—the informal moments that, in a traditional office, happen without planning but are essential for team cohesion.

In remote and hybrid settings, those moments don't happen by accident. Without deliberate effort, relationships stay shallow. People connect only when they have to. And over time, that affects how teams collaborate, share ideas, and solve problems together.

Remote teams also face their own set of challenges—time zone gaps, miscommunication without body language, and a creeping sense of isolation when people rarely interact outside of scheduled meetings. Strong teamwork doesn't come from more meetings. It comes from creating the right conditions for connection.

Here are three simple strategies that can help build those connections into the way your team works:

1. Encourage micro-collaboration

Before team members bring an issue to you, ask them to talk it through with a colleague first—this builds peer connection and shared ownership.

2. Make space for reflection and shared learning

Carve out time for team members to share lessons learned, mentor each other, or reflect on recent work together—it strengthens trust and accelerates growth.

3. Create low-pressure social spaces

Use informal chat channels or recurring casual meetups to give people a way to connect beyond their task list—it keeps the human side of teamwork alive.

Even small efforts to create these touch points can shift the energy in a team—and make remote work feel a lot more connected.

Remote and hybrid teams can absolutely thrive—but not by accident. What works in an office doesn't automatically translate to a virtual setting. To truly collaborate across distance, you have to rethink how your team brainstorms, communicates, and connects.

That means creating space for deep, asynchronous thinking. It means over-communicating on purpose, using the right channels for the right messages. And it means building relationships deliberately, not leaving them to chance.

When you make these shifts, you'll start to see the difference. More engagement. More clarity. More ownership. Remote work isn't a barrier—it's just a different way of working. And with the right approach, it can become one of your team's greatest strengths.

PART 4

COLLABORATIVE DECISIONS

"Whenever you see a successful business, someone once made a courageous decision."

—Peter F. Drucker (1909–2005), Austrian-American management consultant and author

Few things derail a team faster than confusion around decision-making. When no one knows who gets to decide what, progress stalls, resentment builds, and unnecessary conflicts bubble to the surface. Whether you're operating in a rigid hierarchy or a flatter, more flexible setup, the truth is the same across the board: Ask a few team members how decisions are made, and you'll likely get vague answers—or worse, blank stares.

Of course, some decisions are obvious. High-stakes calls—major investments, client negotiations, or strategic shifts—typically sit with senior leadership. On the flip side, each person usually has autonomy over their own workflow and how they manage their day. But what about everything in between?

That's where the fog sets in.

Most teams lack a shared understanding of who owns what decisions. As a result, team members default to escalating problems to their manager—issues they are more than capable of handling themselves. It's not that they're incapable. Quite the opposite. Most teams are full of expertise and on-the-ground knowledge. What they're missing is clarity.

They don't know which decisions they can make independently, which require collaboration, and which need to be escalated. Without a structure, even the most capable people hesitate. And that hesitation costs time, energy, and trust.

In this part of the book, we'll walk through how to bring structure to your team's decision-making. You'll learn how to map out the different types of decisions your team faces, clarify who should make them, and when to involve others. We'll explore proven frameworks that help teams act faster without sacrificing alignment—and how to prioritize effectively when the to-do list feels endless.

When decision-making becomes transparent, something powerful happens: teams stop waiting for permission and start taking ownership. That's the shift from dependency to self-sufficiency. And that's what we're here to build.

CHAPTER 10

BRAVE DECISIONS, BOLD TEAMS

There's a pattern I see with capable, well-intentioned leaders: They think they need to be involved in every decision the team is making.

Not because they want to control everything—but because they've been trained, subtly and over time, to believe they're supposed to. You start with a few early wins, gain responsibility, build a team, and before you know it, you're the person who answers every question, approves every choice, and solves every problem. The team may be growing, but the decision-making hasn't scaled with it. Everything still flows through you.

If that sounds familiar, you're not alone. And you're definitely not failing. But it's worth asking: How much of that is driven by strategy—and how much by fear?

If I don't make this decision, it won't get done right.

My team isn't ready to take this on.

If I delegate too much, people will think I'm not doing anything.

Those thoughts feel practical, even protective. But they're usually something else: fear of losing control, fear of being seen as irrelevant, fear of something slipping through the cracks.

What they create is a leadership bottleneck. You become the central node in every workflow, the answer to every open question. That might feel efficient in the short term—at least everything's getting done—but in the long run, it wears everyone down.

Being at the center of every decision doesn't make you indispensable. It just makes you overloaded—and your team underpowered.

When leaders hold onto too many decisions, the impact isn't always loud or obvious. It builds up quietly in the background—in missed opportunities, in slower execution, in a team that gradually stops thinking for itself.

Here's what tends to happen:

- You become the blocker to progress. Projects slow down waiting for your input.

- Your team loses confidence in their own judgment. If you always decide, why should they try?

- Initiative and creativity decline. People stop bringing new ideas because they assume you already have the answer.

- Ownership fades. Team members do what they're told but don't take responsibility for outcomes.

You stay reactive. Instead of working strategically, you're caught in an endless loop of approvals, clarifications, and decisions.

It's not sustainable. And it's not the kind of leadership that builds a high-performing team.

If your goal is to grow a team that can operate independently, take smart risks, and lead without you in the room, the first step is knowing which decisions are actually yours to make—and which ones you need to let go of.

We'll get to that in the next chapter. But first, we need to talk about what it takes—mentally, emotionally, and practically—to loosen your grip.

There's a version of leadership that's all about stepping up: being the one who makes the tough call, holds the line, takes responsibility when things go sideways. And that matters.

But there's another side of leadership that gets far less attention—and it's just as important. It's the courage to step back.

Not because you don't care. Not because you're disengaged. But because you're building something bigger than yourself.

Delegating decisions isn't abdication. It's a form of empowerment. It means trusting your team to stretch into the uncomfortable space where growth happens.

It's not easy. It takes courage to hand over a decision you could make faster yourself. It takes even more to stay quiet when the team chooses a different approach than you would have. And it requires real discipline to let the team carry the weight of responsibility—and the risk that comes with it.

You're not stepping back because it's easier. You're stepping back because it's necessary. If you want your team to think critically, act with ownership, and grow their capacity, they need room to practice. And that means you need to stop filling the space by default.

You'll still step in when it counts. But if you want to build a team that leads—not just executes—your job isn't to control every decision. It's to build the conditions where good decisions can happen without you.

This is the fear that lingers just under the surface.

If I stop making every decision, will my team think I'm doing nothing?

Will my manager wonder what exactly I contribute?

These are valid concerns. You've likely worked hard to earn your role—and now you're being told to let go of the very things that made you successful.

But here's what's actually happening when you delegate well: You're creating space for your team to lead. You're increasing their engagement, sharpening their thinking, and giving them the chance to solve problems in ways that stretch their capability.

This isn't just a theory—it's grounded in decades of research.

According to Self-Determination Theory[15], developed by psychologists Edward Deci and Richard Ryan, people do their best work—not because they're being pushed, pressured, or micromanaged—but because three core psychological needs are being met:

1. **Autonomy** – They feel ownership over their work and the freedom to make meaningful choices.

2. **Competence** – They believe they're good at what they do and have opportunities to grow.

3. **Relatedness** – They feel part of something bigger than themselves, connected to others, and valued.

These needs aren't luxuries—they're fundamental. When they're met, motivation goes up, engagement deepens, and people put more care and energy into what they're doing.

Delegating decisions—especially the ones with weight and visibility—can activate all three:

- When you give someone real decision-making authority, you're reinforcing their **autonomy**. You're saying, *"You don't just execute the plan—you help shape it."*

- By trusting them to navigate complexity or ambiguity, you signal that you believe in their **competence**—that they have what it takes to figure things out even if they're still learning.

---

[15]   Ryan, Richard & Deci, Edward. (2000). Self-Determination Theory and the Facilitation of Intrinsic Motivation, Social Development, and Well-Being. The American psychologist. 55. 68-78. 10.1037/0003-066X.55.1.68.

- And when decision-making happens within a shared purpose— not just behind closed doors—you build **relatedness**. People feel more invested because their voice helped shape the outcome.

Too often, leaders hold on to decisions thinking they're protecting the team. But what they're really doing is blocking one of the most powerful drivers of motivation: the opportunity to own something that matters.

So the next time you're debating whether to let your team take the lead, remember—delegation isn't just about offloading work. It creates commitment. And that starts when people feel that what they're doing is theirs.

Fear-to-Action Flow

When you're leading a team, there's a particular kind of tension that shows up when you think about letting go of a decision. It might come as hesitation before a meeting, an impulse to jump in with an answer, or a quick, automatic thought: *"I should handle this myself."*

Those moments are often dismissed as instinct. In reality, they're worth paying attention to. They're not always signals to act—but they are signals to pause. Because they often point to fear. Fear of mistakes. Fear of how others will see you. Fear that stepping back might look like disengagement.

The **Fear-to-Action Flow** is a five-step process to help you work through that discomfort and make intentional decisions—either to step in with purpose or step back with confidence. It's especially useful in situations where you're tempted to over-own something simply because it feels safer that way.

Step 1: Notice – Where are you feeling the tension?

The first step is awareness. You don't need to analyze or justify it—just notice that you're feeling uneasy.

Is there a conversation coming up where you feel the urge to speak more than necessary? A decision someone else could make, but you're planning to weigh in anyway? A task you're reluctant to delegate, even though you know someone else could take it?

These are moments worth examining.

Step 2: Name the Fear — What's Underneath the hesitation?

Next, put words to the discomfort. Is it about control? Reputation? Concern for the outcome? Anxiety about how others might perceive you?

Often, the fear is less about the decision itself and more about what the outcome might say about you.

"If they don't handle it well, it'll make me look weak."

"If I'm not the one answering questions, people will wonder what I'm even doing here."

Naming the fear doesn't eliminate it. But it gives you a clearer picture of what's actually driving your actions.

Step 3: Re-anchor – What matters more than protecting yourself?

Once you've identified the fear, take a step back and reconnect with your broader goal.

Is your job to look competent in every moment—or to build a team that doesn't rely on you for everything? Are you protecting your image, or investing in your team's growth?

This is the re-centering point. What principle, value, or long-term purpose is more important than short-term comfort?

"I want to develop leaders, not create dependencies."

"Our credibility as a team comes from shared ownership—not just mine."

Step 4: Reframe – What would courage look like in this situation?

Ask yourself directly: *If I were acting from courage instead of fear, what would I do?*

Would you let someone else take the lead in a high-stakes meeting? Would you trust your team member to present the strategy? Would you stay quiet even when you know the answer—because it's not your turn to speak?

This is not about letting go passively. It's about choosing to let go as a deliberate act of leadership.

Step 5: Act (or Delegate) – Decide how to move forward

Now that you've clarified what's at play, choose what to do. You might decide to keep the decision—but do it intentionally. Or you might step back and give someone else the space to lead.

And if you delegate, do it fully. Don't hover. Don't pre-correct. Let them handle it, and be there afterward to support, debrief, or adjust.

A Real Moment: Learning to Step Back

I remember my first time as a manager. I used to be extremely tense whenever my team members were speaking in meetings. And it wasn't just in the beginning. For five, maybe even seven years, I felt it was my responsibility to respond to every question. I thought I needed to have answers to everything. If I wasn't the one speaking, what would people think? That I was unprepared? That I didn't know what I was doing?

There was one particular meeting that changed things for me. One of my team members was presenting the results of our performance appraisal review to the board. The chair asked a question comparing the data to the previous year's results—and we hadn't included that in the presentation. I knew she wouldn't have the answer. And in that split second, I felt everything inside me tense up. I wanted to jump in and fix it. Say something. Fill the gap.

But I didn't.

She took a breath, looked at the chair, and said, "*I don't have that number at hand, but I'll check and send it to you this afternoon.*"

That was it. And it was enough.

She had built strong relationships with the board. She was respected. She knew how to hold her ground. And by trusting her to lead, I had given her the space to show that.

In that moment, I realized something critical: When you let your team speak for themselves, when you let them take the lead, they don't just perform. They grow. They carry themselves—and they carry you. They're not just backing themselves. They're backing the whole team.

Ever since that moment, I've been able to sit in meetings without the constant urge to take over. Not because the tension is gone entirely—but because I know what that tension means. And I know what's possible when I move through it instead of acting on it.

That's the shift. That's the work.

And that's what the Fear-to-Action Flow is here to help you practice.

Lead with Intention, Not Control

Courage in leadership doesn't always look bold or dramatic. Often, it's quieter than that. It's the choice to stop answering every question. The decision to let someone else speak, even when you're tempted to jump in. The discipline to sit with discomfort and still choose trust.

If you've built your leadership identity around being reliable, responsive, and in control, loosening your grip can feel unfamiliar—maybe even risky. But the truth is, your value doesn't come from being everywhere at once. It comes from building a team that can stand on its own.

Sebastian Gerhardt, Co-Founder and CEO of Flea, has spent years working with engineering teams to help them build stronger cultures and decision-making practices. One of his biggest insights: Organizations often waste the very talent they worked so hard to bring in.

As Sebastian told me, *"It's really startling that companies hire smart people, pay them a lot of money, and then just tell them top-down what to do — instead of using the full power of the team, making them feel heard, and letting them be part of creating solutions."*

Great leadership isn't about having all the answers. It's about creating the conditions where the people you've hired can help find the answers themselves.

(If you want to hear more of Sebastian's insights on building great engineering teams, check out our full conversation on my YouTube channel.)

Letting go of every decision isn't the goal. What matters is deciding which decisions truly need your hand—and which ones are better off with someone else. That shift is what sets great leaders apart: They don't disappear from the process; they redesign it so others can contribute fully.

So if something feels heavy on your plate right now, ask yourself: Is this mine to carry? Or is it time to pass the weight?

That's what it looks like to move forward—on purpose.

In the next chapter, we'll get specific about how to make those calls. You'll learn how to map out decision ownership clearly across your team and how to choose the right approach for each kind of decision. Because once you stop trying to do it all, you'll need a structure to help your team do it well.

CHAPTER 11

WHO DECIDES WHAT—AND HOW TO MAKE IT WORK

"If you're the default decision-maker for everything, your team isn't growing—and you're probably burning out."

That single line captures a reality many leaders live with but rarely name. Decision-making creep is subtle. It builds slowly—through questions routed your way, projects that stall without your sign-off, teammates who pause until they get your OK.

You're making far more decisions than you need to—and probably handling ones your team is fully capable of owning. It's not a question of competence. It's a question of clarity. Who decides? When do we align? When do we just move?

When those lines are blurry, progress slows. People hesitate. Meetings multiply. And you step in again—just to keep things on track. Eventually, that becomes the default. You're reacting, not leading. And your team stays dependent.

This chapter is about breaking that cycle. You'll learn how to build a decision-making strategy that fits your team's context, maturity, and goals.

You'll learn how to:

- Clarify who owns what types of decisions
- Match the right method to the right moment
- Build team confidence and reduce bottlenecks

Because decision rights are a core part of how work gets done. If you've designed workflows and roles, but left decision-making up to chance, your system is only half built. And eventually, that gap shows—through delay, disengagement, and leaders stretched far too thin.

Let's start filling that gap.

Once you recognize that decision-making is slowing your team down, the next move is to bring structure to what often feels like chaos. That starts with a simple question: What kind of decision is this—and who's best positioned to make it?

To help answer that, let's use a model that breaks team decisions into four categories—or zones. Not all decisions are the same, not all of them require the same level of attention, and when you can categorize them, it'll help you agree with the team on how the decisions are going to be made.

The Four Decision Zones:

1. Leader-Owned

These are high-impact decisions that require broad context, strategic alignment, or authority that sits at the leadership level.

Examples: Final hiring decisions, budget approvals, cross-functional trade-offs.

2. Team-Shared

These decisions benefit from multiple perspectives and collective ownership. They affect how the team functions together.

Examples: Team norms, meeting cadence, sprint priorities, shared KPIs.

3. **IC-Owned**

These are decisions best made by individual contributors with specific domain expertise. Speed matters here, and so does autonomy.

Examples: How to approach a task, which tools to use, how to respond to a client issue.

4. **Escalated/Executive**

These involve risk, compliance, or coordination across multiple departments. They go beyond the team's control and require senior input.

Examples: Legal review, data privacy issues, organization-wide changes.

This simple classification gives you and your team a shared vocabulary. It removes guesswork. Instead of reacting to each decision as it comes, you start to design decision-making with intention.

Ok, we know the decision zones, but how do you allocate decisions into them? How can you remove decision ambiguity as much as possible?

To bring more structure, we can use the Decision Delegation Grid (visualized below), which helps assign ownership based on key factors.

This tool gives you and your team a shared framework to define exactly who owns which types of decisions, who contributes, and where collaboration is essential. It has helped many of my clients build a shared operating system that removes hesitation and speeds up execution.

But before you can fill it in, you need a process for deciding who should own what. And that starts with a few strategic filters.

How to Assign Decision Ownership

Every team makes dozens of decisions each week. Some are tactical, others strategic. Some affect only one person's workflow; others ripple across departments. The key is knowing which decisions belong where.

Use these four questions as your guide:

1. What's the impact of the decision?

- If the outcome significantly affects strategy, budget, customers, or other teams, it likely belongs with the leader.

- If the impact is contained within the team—or even better, within one person's role—it can usually be delegated.

2. Who has the most relevant expertise?

- Don't mistake hierarchy for insight. The person closest to the work often has the best judgment call.

- Ask yourself: Who understands the trade-offs best? Who will have to live with the outcome?

3. Does this decision require alignment across the team?

- Some decisions are best made together—like setting priorities, defining workflows, or changing team norms.

- If multiple people will be affected in their day-to-day work, a shared decision usually builds more buy-in and leads to smoother implementation.

4. What's the urgency and risk?

- Fast-moving, low-risk decisions should not clog up leadership time.

- High-risk decisions—legal exposure, reputational impact, customer escalations—often warrant leader ownership or escalation, even if the initial work is delegated.

When you use these questions consistently, assigning decision roles becomes less emotional and more systematic. It also gives your team a logic they can follow, which builds confidence and reduces unnecessary escalations.

The Decision Delegation Grid

To make this approach easy to apply in the flow of work, it helps to visualize how these decisions cluster. For that, we will use Decision Delegation Grid.

A Simple Visual to Support Better Calls

The grid is based on two of the four filters you've already considered:

- **Impact** – How wide or high-stakes is the decision?
- **Expert Knowledge** – How much specialized, technical, or contextual knowledge is needed to make a good call?

Those two dimensions give us a simple, four-zone layout that reflects how most team-level decisions break down:

	High Expert Knowledge	Low Expert Knowledge
High Impact	Team-Shared	Leader-Owned
	Decisions that benefit from broad input and deep expertise. E.g. tool selection, team norms.	Strategic decisions where the leader brings cross-functional context. E.g. budget sign-off, hiring.
Low Impact	Team member-Owned	Delegate or Automate
	Fast, local decisions where the person closest to the work leads.	Repetitive or operational decisions that don't need expertise or debate.

Once you've walked through the four key questions, this visual helps you validate your choice and communicate it clearly to your team.

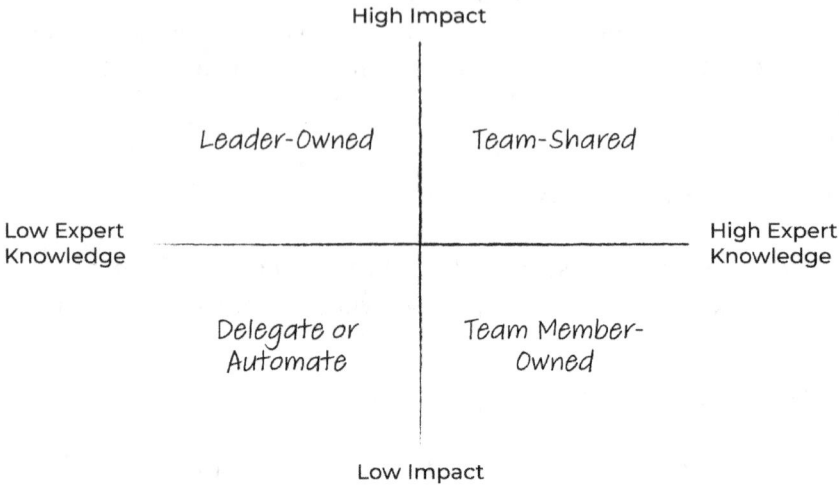

When Escalation Is the Right Move

Not every decision fits neatly inside the grid. Some go beyond your team's scope entirely. That's when it's time to escalate, especially if the decision:

- Involves legal, compliance, or regulatory issues
- Touches multiple teams or departments
- Ties into broader strategic initiatives or budget lines
- Could create reputational or operational risk

When your team understands the difference between a local decision and a cross-functional one, they stop over-escalating and start leading where they can.

Build Shared Understanding

You don't need to publish a chart for every single decision. But once you've walked through this thinking and shared it with your team, it creates a common language. Over time, people will begin to self-sort their decisions—owning what's theirs, collaborating when it makes sense, and flagging what's truly out of scope.

It's not about making fewer decisions. It's about making better ones—in the right place, with the right people, at the right time.

Clarifying who owns a decision is only half the equation. The next question is just as critical: How should that decision actually get made?

There's no universal formula—context matters.

Some decisions benefit from speed. Others need broad alignment. Some call for expert input. Others require creative thinking. When you have a variety of proven decision-making frameworks at hand, you can choose the right method for the moment, so your team knows what's expected and how to move forward. Here are three proven methods that cover a wide range of team decisions. You don't need to use them all. But knowing when to apply each one can save time, increase buy-in, and improve the quality of your decisions.

Nominal Group Technique (NGT)

The Nominal Group Technique is a structured way to gather ideas and make decisions without one voice dominating the room. It's especially useful when you want everyone to contribute—even the quieter voices—and make a collective choice from a range of options.

How it works:

1. Start with a clear problem or question.

2. Everyone silently writes down their ideas. You can easily do it virtually.

3. Ideas are shared one at a time (round-robin style) and written on a board or shared document—without discussion.

4. Once all ideas are listed, the team discusses them for clarity (not for debate). Ask clarifying questions without judgment.

5. Everyone votes privately on their top options. The group then reviews and acts on the highest-ranked ideas.

Best for:

Generating ideas, prioritizing options, and making group decisions when you want equal participation and limited bias.

Use when:

- You're brainstorming solutions to a team-wide challenge.
- You want input from everyone, not just the loudest or most senior.
- You need to quickly converge on a shortlist or next step.

Consensus Building

Consensus building is about reaching decisions that everyone can support even if it's not their first choice. It's slower than other methods, but it builds stronger commitment—especially when the decision affects how the team works together over time.

How it works:

1. Present a proposal or decision area.

2. Open the floor for discussion: gather concerns, ideas, and suggestions. At this point, the main goal is to collect as many ideas or questions a possible.

3. Cluster the groups of questions or concerns into different groups and then start discussing ideas within one group so that the team stays focused on one topic.

4. Work through objections groups by group to find adjustments that bring people closer to agreement. That might take time so

do that only when the design impacts everyone on the team and you need commitment from all the team members.

5. The decision is finalized when everyone agrees it's a direction they can live with and commit to.

Important note:

Consensus does not mean unanimous enthusiasm. It means shared ownership of the outcome—even if not everyone gets exactly what they wanted.

Best for:

Team-wide decisions where buy-in is critical to successful implementation.

Use when:

- You're setting team values, norms, or policies.
- The decision will impact how people work together long-term.
- You need everyone to support the outcome publicly.

Multi-Criteria Decision Analysis (MCDA)

MCDA helps teams make complex decisions by breaking them down into specific criteria. It's a rational, structured method for comparing options when there's no clear winner—and when you're weighing different kinds of trade-offs.

How it works:

1. List your decision options.
2. Identify three to five key criteria (e.g. cost, time, scalability, impact).

3. Assign a weight to each criterion based on its importance.

4. Score each option against each criterion.

5. Multiply the scores by the weights and total them up. The highest-scoring option becomes the leading choice.

Best for:

High-stakes decisions with multiple variables, where logic and clarity are more important than speed.

Use when:

- You're choosing between vendors, tools, or strategic initiatives.
- You want to avoid bias or groupthink.
- The decision has long-term consequences or trade-offs to manage.

These methods don't need to be over-engineered. You can apply them quickly, informally, or even in combination depending on your team's needs. The point isn't to turn every decision into a process—it's to equip your team with enough structure to make decisions confidently, without constantly deferring to you.

When the right person owns the decision—and the right process supports it—you'll spend less time in meetings, more time in motion, and your team will move from hesitation to high performance.

From Decision Chaos to Clarity

FastGrowingCompany Inc. had built its brand on innovation and speed. In just two years, the team had tripled in size, expanded into new markets, and launched multiple product lines. Internally, the company prided itself on being open, flat, and collaborative. "We move fast and we listen to each other," said CEO Alex during all-hands meetings. "No bureaucracy. Everyone's voice matters."

But as the company scaled, cracks started to show—especially in how decisions got made.

Alex remained closely involved in most areas of the business. His passion was contagious, but his influence was hard to ignore. In meetings, his offhand comments often set the direction even when they weren't intended as decisions. In one leadership sync, he mused aloud, "Should we think about pausing work on the onboarding flow and go heavier on integrations?" Heads nodded. No one challenged it. And within a week, teams were shifting priorities—without a real conversation about trade-offs or impact.

Priya, the VP of Engineering, noticed a deeper pattern. Decisions weren't being made in the open. They were happening in fragments—one-on-one Slack messages, side conversations, casual remarks. Sometimes decisions got reversed because another executive hadn't been consulted. Other times, a decision would be treated as final even though key people weren't in the room. More than once, Priya's team had to walk back work they had already started—burning time and eroding trust.

It all came to a head when a cross-functional initiative derailed weeks before launch. Multiple teams had been working under different assumptions about scope and ownership. At the post-mortem, frustration spilled over. "The biggest problem," Priya said, "is that no one knows who's supposed to be in the loop—or when a decision is actually final."

Alex was surprised. "But we've always kept things open. I've never stopped anyone from speaking up."

The VP of Customer Success added, "That's true—but if you're not part of the right conversation at the right time, it doesn't matter. The way we're deciding things isn't inclusive. It's unpredictable."

What became clear in that moment was this: The company wasn't lacking in collaboration. It was lacking in structure. No one wanted to slow things down with process. But the absence of a shared decision-making strategy was doing just that.

Over the next few weeks, the executive team worked together to shift how they made decisions. They started by mapping out the decisions they encountered most often—strategic shifts, hiring choices, product priorities, operational changes—and used the four-question framework from this chapter to clarify ownership.

- What's the impact of the decision?
- Who has the relevant expertise?
- Does it require alignment across functions?
- What's the urgency and risk?

Then they took it one step further. They agreed that before any significant decision moved forward, they would walk it through the Decision Delegation Grid. Not just to clarify ownership but to ensure they had included everyone affected by the outcome. That meant:

- No making decisions in side channels if others were going to execute them
- No final calls without the right expertise in the room
- No deep discussions unless all stakeholders were present

This way, the team has managed to create predictability and respect in how they worked together.

Six months later, the difference was visible. Meetings became more focused. Cross-functional decisions became easier to navigate. Teams stopped waiting for direction—and started asking smarter questions about how decisions should be made.

Alex still had a strong voice in the company. But now, it was clear when he was offering input and when he was making a call. The executive team had found a way to balance inclusion with clarity—and in doing so, they made faster decisions that stuck.

They hadn't lost their agility. They'd grown into it.

How to Introduce Decision-making in Your Team

You don't need a reorg to fix decision-making. But you do need a shared understanding and to make sure you team is clear on how decisions are made from now on.

Here's how you can roll this out without overwhelming your people or slowing the work.

Start Small and Real

1. **Pick one upcoming decision.**

Choose something meaningful but manageable. A new project scope. A customer escalation. A hiring decision. Use this as your test case.

2. **Ask the four framing questions.**

As a team, walk through:

- What's the impact?
- Who has the relevant expertise?
- Does this require alignment?
- What's the urgency and risk?

3. **Place the decision on the Delegation Grid.**

Use the grid to clarify:

- Who should own it
- Who needs to be involved
- Whether this stays with the team or needs to be escalated

4. **Choose the right method to make the call.**

Based on the decision type, use one of the three methods:

- NGT for idea generation
- Consensus for team-wide alignment
- MCDA for complex trade-offs

5. **Make the decision and debrief.**

Once the decision is made, take five minutes to reflect:

- Did the process work?
- Was ownership clear?
- What would we change next time?

6. **Repeat and scale.**

Don't wait to perfect the model. Use it again for the next decision. Soon, your team will internalize the logic—and start using it without prompting.

As a leader you don't need to control every decision. With the methods from this chapter, you'll build a system your team can trust—even when you're not in the room.

CHAPTER 12

FROM FIREFIGHTING TO FOCUS: HOW TOP TEAMS PRIORITIZE

"Everything's a priority." That's the feeling teams have nowadays. And that is also a recipe for burnout. Tasks are falling from everywhere, new organizational initiatives require attention—those multiple demands and constant changes create an ongoing sense of urgency, as well as no clarity at all about what to do first.

My bet is that you and your team know exactly what I'm talking about, and you find yourselves juggling 10 different "top priorities" way too often. And again, as I mentioned many times before in this book, the challenge lies in a lack of clarity. Teams are working hard. They're working constantly. But without a shared understanding of what matters most, they're spinning their wheels and slowly grinding down.

This kind of prioritization paralysis comes because of different reasons. Here's what typically drives it:

Constant change

When things change in the organization, the reasons behind the change and the shift in priorities don't always flow smoothly to every team and even every leader in the organization. The bigger the organization is, the bigger those communication gaps are.

Recency bias

As a byproduct of this constant change, teams often focus on the most recent initiative, putting everything else aside. Since everyone is talking about the "next big change," chances are that becomes the priority... for now. And then comes the new change, the backlog of unfinished tasks grows bigger, and priorities shift with no visible results.

Pressure to Say "Yes"

Sometimes the biggest obstacle is cultural. When saying "yes" is seen as being helpful, responsive, or a team player, declining low-priority work can feel risky. Teams end up overloaded, trying to meet every request instead of advancing strategic goals. These traps aren't signs of a lazy or disengaged team. More often than not, they're symptoms of a well-meaning group trying to do too much with too little direction. If you don't build a shared system for prioritizing, urgency will decide for you—and urgency has terrible judgment.

Enhanced Eisenhower Matrix for Teams

If urgency keeps hijacking your team's focus, you need a shared way to decide what truly matters—and what doesn't. This is where most teams struggle. Everyone agrees they're too busy. But ask what to drop, delay, or deprioritize, and things get quiet.

That's why we use the Eisenhower Matrix—a powerful decision-making tool for teams. On its own, the matrix is a simple framework: Sort your tasks by urgency and importance into four quadrants.

You've probably seen it before:

- Do (Urgent and Important)
- Plan (Not Urgent but Important)
- Question (Urgent but Not Important)
- Drop (Neither Urgent nor Important)

	Urgent	Not Urgent
Important	Do	Plan
Not Important	Question	Drop

I'll be honest with you—ever since I learned the tool, it never worked for me the way it was supposed to. Why? Because while sorting tasks into those four quadrants, most of them landed in the Urgent and Important section. Everything was important, and since I never had enough time to complete them all—everything was also urgent.

Everything feels urgent when you're under pressure.

The good thing is that over time, I managed to hack the classic Eisenhower Matrix, and now I'll give you five tricks that make this tool work every time—the Enhanced Eisenhower Matrix.

Here's how to make it work.

1. Find the Center of Gravity

Start by noticing where most of your tasks land. Are they clustered in "Do"? That's your first clue. We are not forcing an even distribution; what we need is to challenge the assumption that all of those tasks are equally urgent and important. Talk about why that quadrant is overloaded. What's driving the sense of urgency? Is it real, or just playing safe by putting everything in the Do section?

Prompt the team:

"Are these tasks truly urgent and important... compared to each other?"

That question alone often reshuffles the list.

2. Reflect the Level of Effort

Once you've placed the tasks, go back and estimate the level of effort for each one. Small, Medium, Large, Extra Large—whatever works for your team. Visually label or color-code the effort directly on the matrix. This helps surface the hidden cost of your to-dos.

Because here's the thing: Not all important work is equally feasible right now. Something might belong in "Do" on paper—but if it's an extra large lift and your team is underwater, you'll need to revisit the timing or rescope it.

Ask:

"Can we realistically take this on right now, given the effort it requires?"

3. Score by Impact

Now bring in another layer—impact. Score each task from 1 to 5 based on how much it moves the needle on your team's actual goals. A task with a 5 means significant progress; a 1 means minimal difference.

This step is where things often shift. That task someone has been championing? Maybe it's not as high-impact as assumed. Or a quiet but strategic task suddenly rises in importance. This reframes the conversation around value, not noise. Any task with low impact score in a "Do" section should be moved to "Plan" or "Question" quadrants.

4. Apply the 80/20 Rule

Only roughly 20% of tasks often produce 80% of the results. Look at the tasks in the "Important" sections. Which few are likely to drive most of the results? These are your 20%—the vital few that deserve focus. Mark them visibly.

Teams are often surprised by how few tasks actually qualify. That's the point. You don't need to do more to make progress—you need to do the right things.

5. Set Limits for the "Do" Quadrant

Finally, draw a line. Literally. Cap the number of tasks that can live in the "Do" quadrant—three to five, max. This forces hard decisions and builds alignment fast. If something doesn't make the cut, move it to "Plan" or "Question."

We are not being rigid here. The number of tasks you leave in the "Do" section needs to be the team's decision. And after all, the number itself is not that important—what matters is that team members start to challenge assumptions and critically evaluate things they used to consider important by default. That's how teams learn to fight back against the "everything is urgent" reflex.

Use all of these tricks together or pick those that resonate most with your team or your context. The most important thing is that when you start having those conversations, you're not just sorting cards—you're building the muscle of the team's shared judgment.

When and How to Use It

So when should you use the Enhanced Eisenhower Matrix?

Don't wait until your team is drowning. This tool works best as a recurring conversation—not a crisis response. If you only pull it out when the wheels are coming off, you'll reinforce the idea that prioritization is a fire drill. Instead, normalize it. Make it a part of how your team works, plans, and adjusts together. Make it part of the agenda for your Implementer Execution-Focused Roundtable (see Chapter 8 for more details).

Here are the moments when it makes the biggest difference:

- **When your team is overloaded:** If people are constantly firefighting and complaining about bandwidth, use the matrix to bring visibility to what's on the plate—and what needs to come off.

- **When priorities keep shifting:** If your team is whiplashed by changing direction, the matrix helps anchor your focus. It offers a visual reset so you're not just reacting—you're choosing.

- **When there's tension about what matters most:** If debates are heating up about where to focus, the matrix surfaces assumptions and creates space for alignment. You're not arguing about tasks—you're aligning on value.

- **When you want to work smarter, not just harder:** Even high-performing teams fall into the trap of doing too much. A regular prioritization habit helps teams protect their time and energy for what really moves the needle.

In short: don't treat prioritization as a one-off activity. Build it into your team's rhythm. A short monthly session can do more to align your team than any number of status updates or check-ins. Once your team gets used to working this way, the process becomes second nature. You'll spend less time reacting—and more time making progress.

Facilitation Tips: Making It Work in the Real World

Whether you're running this exercise in-person or remotely, here are a few practical tips to make sure your prioritization session runs smoothly and gets real traction.

Keep it Under 60 Minutes

Don't overdesign it. Start with a short, focused session. Dump all the tasks the team has, and then limit the number of tasks you review closely (aim for 15 to 20 max, depending on how aligned your team is at the moment). The more you're used to discussing priorities, the easier it goes each time.

Run It Virtually with Ease

Use a collaborative digital whiteboard like Miro, Mural, or Microsoft Whiteboard. Set up the four-quadrant grid in advance and pre-load your team's task list as sticky notes. Assign colors or tags for effort and impact. Keep screen sharing on so everyone stays engaged. (Go to my website dariarudnik.com and use the pre-designed Miro template for your Enhanced Eisenhower Matrix team session.)

Get Full Participation

Don't let the loudest voices take over. Use breakout rooms if the group is large—have smaller groups sort the tasks, then reconvene to compare results. Ask open-ended questions to draw quieter team members in:

> "What's one task here that feels misplaced?"

> "Which one of these are we doing out of habit, not strategy?"

Make It a Habit, Not a Hail Mary

Put it on the calendar every month. Have shorter sessions at your weekly meetings. Create a collaboration board where everyone can leave comments or questions, as well as respond to them. A recurring prioritization ritual makes it easier to spot misalignment before it becomes a problem.

From Burnout to Focus

When I started working with the executive team of a small VC fund, they were already deep in firefighting mode. Their days were a blur of investor calls, program development, back-and-forths with regulators, and trying to hold their internal teams together. Every conversation started the same way: *"We're buried. Everything's urgent. And no one else seems to be keeping up."*

On paper, this was a sharp, high-capacity team. But in practice, they were scattered, reactive, and increasingly frustrated with one another. Their backlog was endless, and so was the tension. Everyone felt like they were constantly cleaning up someone else's mess—and no one had the time to zoom out and ask: *What are we actually trying to accomplish?*

In one of our early coaching sessions, we decided to make the problem visible. We asked everyone to list every active task on their plate—big or small, strategic or tactical. The screen filled up fast. Client-related tasks like "fundraising strategy" and "monthly reporting to LPs" sat alongside "define onboarding process," "CRM cleanup," "answer regulator requests," and "launch newsletter." At first glance, everything seemed important. But there was no structure. Just a tangle of scattered tasks across color-coded branches, each one pulling the team in a different direction.

What we discovered in that session changed everything.

Discovery #1: Related work was fragmented across people.

One team member was drafting investor updates. Another was handling CRM outreach. A third was preparing a fund deck. All of it was part of the same investor engagement flow—but it was being split in pieces, creating duplication and missed connections. Once we saw that, it was clear the work should be clustered by function, not by person. Assigning entire workstreams to one owner created immediate clarity—and reduced the mental overhead of constant coordination.

Discovery #2: Some tasks didn't belong right now.

As we scored impact and effort, the team quickly spotted a handful of "interesting but optional" projects that had crept onto the list. Tasks like "launch newsletter" or "look into ESG metrics" were passion projects—worth exploring, but not essential to the fund's short-term strategic goals. Seeing them visually ranked against more critical work made it easier to say: *Not now. Not never. Just not now.* Postponing them freed up space for what mattered.

Discovery #3: Strategy was getting lost in the noise.

This was the most powerful insight of all. When the team stepped back, they realized their actual strategic priorities—like refining the fund's investment thesis, hiring a new analyst, or repositioning to differentiate from competitors—were being consistently pushed aside. These weren't unclear goals. They just weren't showing up in the weekly workflow. Instead, they lived in the "someday" pile while the team stayed stuck in reactive mode.

Seeing that disconnect laid the groundwork for change. The team made a conscious decision to pull one of those initiatives—redefining their value proposition to investors—into the "Plan" quadrant. They carved out protected time each week to work on it as a group. That one move shifted their mindset. For the first time in months, they weren't just responding. They were building.

By the end of the session, the list hadn't shrunk. But the energy in the room had changed. The team capped their "Do Now" items to just five, reassigned overlapping tasks, and deferred three experimental projects that were dragging down focus. They didn't just walk away with a cleaner matrix. They walked away with a shared lens.

The team changed how they handled priorities—making it a shared responsibility instead of something each person struggled with alone. They committed to check their priority matrix monthly, adjust their work based on strategic goals, and call it out when emergency requests threatened to derail their planned work.

This move, from chaotic activity to deliberate focus, did more than boost productivity. It began repairing the team's trust in each other.

Beyond the Matrix: Prioritization as Team Culture

The matrix works great as a tool—but real, lasting change comes from shifting your culture.

Many teams see prioritization as just a tactical exercise. Something done during planning sessions. Or when time gets tight. Or when chaos reaches a breaking point.

But teams that really nail it weave prioritization into their everyday habits.

This means prioritization happens beyond workshops—it shows up in conversations, planning, and daily collaboration. It becomes how your team naturally thinks about what matters, where time goes, and what deserves focus.

Here's how to make this happen:

Build these questions into your team's regular rhythm:

- What's most valuable right now?
- What can we drop?
- Where should we spend our time this week?

You won't need a formal matrix every time. What you do need is a shared instinct to step back, look at the big picture, and reassess. This only works when people feel they can question priorities—and when adjusting plans as circumstances change becomes normal.

One clear sign of a healthy team? When someone feels comfortable saying:

"I don't think this is worth our effort right now. Should we rethink this?"

It's not about rigidity. It's about being deliberate.

The real win isn't just a cleaner to-do list. It's building a team that stays focused together—even when everything around them gets crazy and demanding.

PART 5

KNOWLEDGE SHARING

"Everybody is smarter than anybody."

—Carl Sandburg (1878–1967), American poet, biographer, and journalist

You've made it to Part 5—Knowledge Sharing. By this point, your team has defined its purpose, strengthened connections with stakeholders, integrated the way it works, and clarified how it makes decisions. What comes next is making sure all of that sticks—and evolves. This part is about helping your team grow together by learning together.

Research[16] consistently shows that knowledge sharing and team learning are essential to building high-performing, self-sufficient teams. In remote or hybrid environments, these practices are even more critical. When teams learn openly and regularly, they strengthen trust, improve coordination, and unlock deeper collaboration. They don't just operate well—they improve how they operate over time.

---

[16] Alsharo, Mohammad & Gregg, Dawn & Ramirez, Ronald. (2016). Virtual team effectiveness: The role of knowledge sharing and trust. Information & Management. 54. 10.1016/j.im.2016.10.005.

The best teams embed knowledge into their routines. They make feedback normal, tackle tough conversations early, and take time to reflect—on results, relationships, and how they're working together.

In this part, we'll break down the three core pillars of effective knowledge sharing:

- **Feedback.** High-performing teams don't wait for feedback—they ask for it. They give it generously, whether it's praise or constructive direction. They recognize each other's impact, support learning, and make feedback part of how they move forward. And they don't stop at the team boundary—they seek input from internal clients, cross-functional partners, and key stakeholders to strengthen collaboration across the organization.

- **Constructive Conflict.** These teams don't avoid disagreement—they engage with it. They create space for differing opinions and ensure those conversations stay focused on ideas, not personalities. By surfacing issues early and resolving tensions directly, they reduce the risk of conflict debt and keep trust intact.

- **Reflection.** Finally, they build in regular opportunities to reflect—on both their outcomes and how they got there. They review what worked, what didn't, and what could be improved. They revisit their norms, communication, and decision-making habits with the same rigor they apply to their project goals.

When teams do all three—seek feedback, engage in healthy conflict, and reflect regularly—they don't just react to problems. They learn, adapt, and grow together.

In the next chapters, we'll look at how to build these habits into your team's rhythm. You'll find practical tools, feedback frameworks, and step-by-step guides for retrospectives and reflection. The goal isn't perfection—it's progress, shared openly.

Let's dig in.

CHAPTER 13

ASK BETTER QUESTIONS, GET REAL FEEDBACK

Feedback is one of the most powerful drivers of growth—both for individuals and for teams. When done well, it strengthens relationships, accelerates learning, and improves performance across the board. It's not just a leadership tool. It's a team development strategy.

And people want it.

Research[17] from Harvard Business Review shows that 57% of employees prefer corrective feedback over praise. Seventy-two percent believe their performance would improve if their managers provided more of it. Even more striking: 92% agree that negative, redirecting feedback—if delivered appropriately—is effective at improving performance.

High-performing teams don't wait around for feedback to be handed to them. They ask for it. They give it generously—to each other, across functions, and up and down the hierarchy. They recognize contributions, address issues early, and use feedback to stay aligned and keep improving.

---

[17] Your Employees Want the Negative Feedback You Hate to Give https://hbr.org/2014/01/your-employees-want-the-negative-feedback-you-hate-to-give

And they don't limit that practice to individuals. They ask how the team is working, too.

But here's the problem: most feedback requests fall flat.

Some think it's because people don't want to help. But even when they do, the way feedback is usually requested doesn't work. Questions like "Do you have any feedback for me?" or "How am I doing?" sound open and thoughtful—but they're too vague to generate a meaningful response. The person on the receiving end doesn't know what you're really asking, what part of your work you want to hear about, or whether it's safe to be fully honest. So they default to the safe answer: "You're doing great." Or nothing at all.

That's the first gap—asking in a way that's too broad, too generic, or too awkward to answer honestly.

The second, and arguably more damaging, is that teams rarely ask for feedback about their collective work.

We're used to feedback as a tool for personal growth. We ask our manager how we're performing. We reach out to a colleague to ask how we handled a conversation or project. But few teams pause to ask, "*How are we doing together?*" They don't solicit input on their collaboration, communication, or shared decision-making. As a result, underlying tensions go unaddressed, inefficiencies become habits, and team dynamics stagnate—even when everyone's individually performing well.

Both of these gaps—vague individual feedback requests and the absence of team-level feedback—prevent teams from learning. And when teams don't learn, they don't grow.

And that's what we're going to fix.

When you read this chapter, you'll get the language, structure, and tools to start asking for feedback in a way that works. You'll learn how to ask targeted questions that invite real insight, how to bring feedback into your team's rhythm, and how to shift from backward-looking evaluation to forward-focused improvement.

Let's start with three types of feedback you can ask for to get valuable insights.

Three Types of Feedback Requests

One of my clients once said, "Most senior leaders in our company don't help me grow. When I ask for feedback, they don't give any specific information on what I need to improve. They just keep asking me what *I* want to work on. But I honestly don't know—and I don't know how to figure it out."

That's a common challenge, especially for high performers. You know you want to grow, but you're not sure what to focus on. And when the people around you don't offer anything concrete, you're left stuck in a loop—waiting for insight that never arrives.

Well, you don't need to have all the answers before you can ask a good question.

The key is to give the person you're asking something specific to respond to. That doesn't mean you need a detailed development plan. It just means you need a frame—something that focuses their attention and lowers the pressure of trying to guess what you want.

Below are three types of feedback requests that make it easier to get actionable input even when you're not sure exactly what you're trying to develop. Each one targets a different context—but all three help create clarity, reduce awkwardness, and lead to better conversations.

1. Skill-Specific Feedback

When you're working on a behavior or capability—or even just testing out a new approach—this kind of feedback helps you zoom in on one element and learn how others perceive it.

You can use it to get input on presentation style, communication habits, delegation, meeting presence—anything that's visible in your day-to-day work.

Example:

"I'm working on being more concise when I present updates. After today's meeting, could you let me know if I was clear and to the point?"

Even if you're not actively working on something specific, choosing *one area* to ask about often surfaces insights you didn't know you needed.

2. Event-Based Feedback

You don't need a long-term goal to ask for useful feedback. Sometimes the best moment to learn is right after a meeting, a conversation, or a presentation—when the experience is fresh.

This type of request anchors the feedback to a specific moment. It's a great option when you're experimenting, stepping into a new situation, or just curious how something landed.

Example:

"I tried a new approach in today's client call. I'd love to know what landed well and what could've been stronger."

Because you're asking about a moment rather than a general trait, people can give sharper, more immediate feedback—without overthinking it.

3. Future-Focused Feedback

But one of my favorite ways of asking for feedback is focusing it on the future. People generally don't like to say negative things to someone's face—especially if it's someone they like or regularly interact with. So instead of asking them about how you did in the past, ask what you can do better in the future.

That's the idea behind Future-Focused Feedback—instead of asking for an assessment of your past performance, you ask for suggestions that could help you improve going forward. This lowers defensiveness, removes judgment, and focuses the conversation on learning and action.

Example:

"Next time we run a workshop like this, what's one thing you think I could do differently to make it more engaging?"

Future-Focused Feedback is especially powerful when you're not sure what you need to improve—it invites others to offer ideas without critiquing your past.

When you use more specific requests for feedback, you'll get better responses that are actionable and will help you grow. They also make it easier for your peers, team members, and stakeholders to help you, because they know exactly what you're asking for and how to respond.

Normalize the Ask

Getting feedback once is helpful. But to build a real CLICK team that is autonomous, engaged, and effective, feedback needs to be a part of the culture.

If you want to build a self-sufficient team, feedback needs to move in all directions—not just from leader to team member. Everyone should feel empowered to ask for feedback from their peers, their manager, and the team as a whole. That only happens when feedback-seeking becomes a shared norm.

There are two critical contexts where feedback should flow consistently: within the team and across teams (from stakeholders and partners).

Let's start with the team itself.

Team members should be regularly asking each other for feedback—not just when something goes wrong but as part of how they learn and improve together. That includes giving and requesting feedback after meetings, during 1:1s, or at the end of key projects. And as a leader, you need to model that behavior by asking your own team for feedback on your leadership and how you're supporting them.

Of course, that can feel uncomfortable at first—especially in teams where psychological safety is still being built. One of the best ways to lower the barrier is to create structure around the feedback process. The more intentional and repeatable it feels, the safer it becomes.

Here's a simple method that helps you receive honest, constructive input from your team—even when people are hesitant to speak up directly.

Anonymous Feedback Rounds: A Simple Session You Can Run This Week

Here's how it works:

1. **Anonymous Notes**

In your next team meeting, ask everyone to anonymously respond to a few open questions:

- What do we need to change to be a better team?
- How can we better support each other?
- What's one thing stopping us from being the great team we can be?

2. **Offline or Online**

Collect responses using physical cards (in person) or a shared online board (remote). Make sure you submit your own response as well.

3. **Shuffle and Distribute**

Mix the responses and hand them out randomly to the team.

4. **Advocate for a Point**

Each person reads the response they received and presents it as if it were their own. Invite others to add if they feel strongly about the same point.

5. **Vote and Create an Action Plan**

Once all points have been shared, vote as a group on the top two to three themes to address. Assign owners and create a follow-up plan.

This method helps you get honest responses. It also kickstarts a culture of open reflection and shared responsibility. When used consistently, people become more open to giving feedback and also to receiving it. It builds momentum toward a high-performance mindset, where feedback isn't personal—it's just how the team gets better.

Getting Feedback from Stakeholders

The second critical area where feedback often gets overlooked is *outside the team*—from internal clients, cross-functional partners, and other stakeholders.

Too often, we assume that only the team leader should be gathering this kind of input. But in self-sufficient teams, everyone takes responsibility for learning how the team is showing up across the organization. If you're regularly collaborating with another team, you don't need to wait for your manager to collect that feedback—you can go ask for it directly.

There are a few simple ways to make stakeholder feedback part of your team's regular learning process:

- Set up a short meeting with a partner team to ask how collaboration is going.
- Send a short feedback questionnaire to stakeholders after a major project.
- Ask for Future-Focused Feedback: "What's one thing we could do differently next time to make our work together smoother?"

As a team leader, you can support this in two ways:

- Model it by sending out regular stakeholder check-ins yourself.
- Encourage your team members to do the same with the teams they partner with most often.

Here's a tip: If your team provides a service or product internally (like reporting, project support, or tech tools), it's especially important to treat your stakeholders as *clients*. Their input is essential to improving how your team delivers—and how it's perceived.

Feedback Request Email Template (Leader → Other teams)

Subject: Quick request for feedback on how our teams are working together

Hi [Name],

I'd really appreciate your input on how our teams are collaborating. We're looking at ways to strengthen our cross-functional work and I'd love to hear your perspective on what's working well—and what could be improved.

If you have a few minutes, could you respond to the questions below? You can keep it brief—whatever's top of mind is perfect.

1. What's working well in how our teams collaborate?
2. What's one thing we could do differently to make collaboration smoother or more effective?
3. Is there anything we're doing (or not doing) that creates friction or slows you down?
4. Anything else you'd like us to know?

You can reply directly to this email or drop thoughts in this [link to form or shared doc, if using one].

Thanks so much for taking the time—we really value your input.

Best,

[Your Name]

[Your Role]

You don't need to wait for a case or a problem to ask for feedback. Proactive feedback requests show that your team is committed to continuous improvement—and that you care about the relationships that make your work possible.

Moving beyond the "Good Job"

When Paul was promoted into a senior leadership role, he was excited—but also realistic. He knew that leading other managers would be a different challenge from managing individual contributors. He also knew that feedback would be essential to his growth. What he didn't expect was how hard it would be to get any.

His manager was supportive—but stretched thin. In their check-ins, feedback often sounded like, "Keep doing what you're doing," or "You're doing great." His peers and direct reports offered similar encouragement. It wasn't that they were avoiding him—it's that they didn't know what to say. And Paul wasn't giving them anything specific to respond to.

"I kept getting stuck," Paul told me. "People would ask what I wanted feedback on, and honestly, I didn't know. That's what I was hoping *they* could tell me."

This is where many leaders get stuck—waiting for others to offer insight without realizing they need to shape the question. So we worked with Paul and he shifted his approach.

Instead of asking for "feedback," he began to ask about specific moments and clear behaviors. After team meetings, he'd message a peer and ask,

"I'm trying to get better at giving updates that are short and strategic. In today's meeting, did it feel like I hit the right balance, or was there anything I could tighten up?"

In 1:1s, he'd use future-focused questions with his team and his boss:

"Next time I'm running a strategy session like that, what's one thing I could do differently to get more input from the room?"

The shift was immediate. People knew what he wanted. They felt safe offering suggestions. And he had something he could actually use.

But Paul didn't stop with his own growth. He knew that for his team to become more self-sufficient, feedback needed to flow across the team—not just to him. So he introduced a lightweight practice during their monthly team meeting: a five-minute "What's working / What's not" round. No judgment, just observations. They started sharing small tensions early— before they turned into real problems.

Then he went one step further.

Paul built a short questionnaire to gather feedback from their most important stakeholders—internal partners his team supported on a regular basis. It included questions like:

- What's working well in how we support you and your team?
- What's one thing we could change to improve our collaboration?
- Where do you see opportunities for us to add more value?

He sent it out to a few key partners. The responses were different— some were still very generic, some were more specific, and one even told Paul something he didn't know about his team: One of the team members had supported another team's project in their extra time without asking for reward or recognition.

But something unexpected happened, too.

One of the teams that received Paul's questionnaire decided to adapt it for themselves. They used it to gather feedback from their own stakeholders. Then another team picked it up. Soon, a few groups across the company were running similar feedback rounds, sharing learnings and improving collaboration beyond their own silos.

Paul hadn't just changed how *he* asked for feedback—he'd raised the bar for how teams gave and received it across the organization.

What to Take Away

Feedback is one of the fastest and simplest ways to grow, both as an individual and as a team.

In this chapter, we've looked at why getting useful feedback is hard and what you can do to change that. We've talked about the difference between asking generally and asking with intention. We've shared ways to request feedback from peers, from your team, and from stakeholders outside your immediate group. We looked at future-focused feedback as a way to shift from judgment to growth. And we saw how leaders like Paul built feedback habits that didn't just help their team—they started a ripple effect across the company.

Here's what to remember: Feedback accelerates development, but it also does something deeper. It strengthens trust. When you ask someone for feedback, you show that you value their perspective. When they give it—and you act on it—it builds a connection. That loop creates energy and momentum. You learn faster, together.

Strong teams don't just work alongside each other. They help each other improve. And they don't stop there. When teams actively exchange feedback across functions, they build something even more powerful: a culture of mutual learning, shared accountability, and deep relationships. That's what makes great teams click—and what makes the entire system stronger.

So don't wait for the right moment or the perfect phrasing. Start asking. Start learning. And help your team make feedback a habit that fuels everything they do.

CHAPTER 14

PAY OFF YOUR CONFLICT DEBT

One of the most common misconceptions leaders hold is this: If there's no visible conflict, the team must be working well.

It's easy to fall into that trap. I've been there. Meetings are smooth. People are polite. Everyone agrees. And on the surface, things look aligned. But when a team consistently avoids disagreement, it's rarely a sign of high performance. More often, it's a signal that important conversations aren't happening.

The hard truth is this:

- When consensus is too easy, innovation slows down.
- When disagreement never shows up, it usually means psychological safety is low.
- And when positivity is constant, concerns are often being masked.

In self-sufficient teams, conflict is expected and accepted as a natural occurrence, and is consequently managed well. Disagreement isn't seen as a threat to relationships, but as a natural and necessary part of doing meaningful work together. These teams challenge each other's ideas without turning conflict of ideas into conflict between people.

CLICK teams don't view friction as failure. They view it as fuel for growth.

If a team isn't debating, questioning assumptions, or pushing back on each other's thinking, it's unlikely they're doing their best work.

The problem is, when teams avoid conflict—even unintentionally—they accumulate what we call conflict debt. It's the build-up of unresolved issues, unspoken frustrations, and withheld feedback that slowly undermines performance. Like financial debt, conflict debt compounds over time. And the longer it goes unaddressed, the more damaging—and costly—it becomes.

In this chapter, we'll look at how to recognize the signs of conflict debt, how to create space for honest conversations, and how to help your team move from silent alignment to productive disagreement. Because what your team isn't saying might be holding them back far more than you realize.

Here's how you can spot it on your team—by noticing five common symptoms of conflict debt:

1. **Silent Consensus**

When decisions are made quickly and no one asks questions or raises objections, it's worth pausing. Are people truly aligned, or are they withholding concerns because they think it's safer not to speak up? And even when people are truly aligned, the lack of questions is alarming because no one can have the same level of information on every decision the team is making.

2. **Emotional Leakage**

Tension doesn't disappear—it just finds other ways to surface. If you notice sarcasm, passive-aggressive comments, or a sharp shift in tone when certain topics come up, those are signs that something's been left unspoken. Try to notice verbal and non-verbal signals that tell you there's something there that we need to have the courage to bring to light.

3. **Low Feedback Activity**

If people rarely ask for feedback, or if feedback only flows from the top down, it's a sign that open communication isn't fully established. Healthy teams exchange input regularly, not just during formal reviews.

4. **Lack of Ownership**

When team members bring their concerns only to the manager—rather than addressing them directly with each other—it signals a breakdown in trust or accountability. Feedback becomes hierarchical instead of mutual. People avoid talking to each other so they don't have to have difficult and honest conversations.

5. **"We're Fine" Culture**

When the team insists everything is fine, even in the face of missed goals, declining morale, or rising tension, it often points to avoidance. A culture that avoids discomfort will eventually avoid growth.

These signals don't always mean there's a crisis. But they are worth paying attention to—especially if you're hearing them repeatedly or noticing them across different areas of the team's work.

You don't need drama to have a conflict problem. All it takes is a pattern of issues that remain unspoken—and unresolved.

Is Your Team Carrying Conflict Debt? A Self-Check for Leaders

Use the statements below to evaluate your team. If you find yourself nodding to several, it's a strong signal that your team may be carrying unresolved conflict—and it's time to address it.

1. Team members rarely ask clarifying questions or challenge proposals during meetings.
2. Most discussions end in agreement—but often without real debate.

3. I find out about tensions through side conversations, not in the room.

4. When concerns are raised, they're directed at me, not discussed peer-to-peer.

5. People are quick to agree publicly but raise doubts privately.

6. We tend to focus on delivering tasks, not on how we're working together.

7. Feedback feels like a formal event—not something we exchange naturally.

8. There's no regular space where the team reflects on our dynamic or collaboration.

9. Team members hesitate to bring up difficult topics unless asked directly.

10. Even when something clearly didn't go well, we rarely talk about what needs to change.

You don't need to check every box for conflict debt to exist. Even a few of these patterns—especially if they persist—can point to conversations that are missing, relationships that need repair, or norms that need rethinking.

The good news is that conflict debt can be addressed. But it starts with creating the right environment: one where people feel safe enough to speak up.

Create Conditions for Safe Conflict

If your team isn't talking about what's not working, at some point, it might seem like they don't care. Sometimes that's true, but even then, it all starts with not trusting that it's safe to speak up.

You can't pay conflict debt just by asking better questions or running a feedback session. What you need to focus on first is building trust—not just between individuals but across the whole team system. And you need it on all five levels of trust[18].

You can think of trust in teams as a pyramid—a layered process of building the conditions for healthy challenge, honest feedback, and real collaboration. The higher a team moves up this trust pyramid, the more able they are to engage in difficult conversations without shutting down or turning on each other.

The Levels of Team Trust

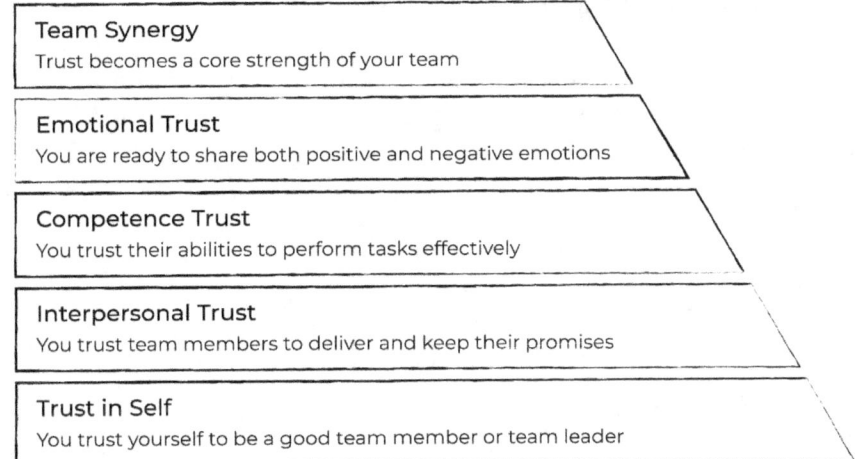

Team Synergy
Trust becomes a core strength of your team

Emotional Trust
You are ready to share both positive and negative emotions

Competence Trust
You trust their abilities to perform tasks effectively

Interpersonal Trust
You trust team members to deliver and keep their promises

Trust in Self
You trust yourself to be a good team member or team leader

Level 1: Self-Trust

This is where it starts. When team members trust themselves, they're more likely to take ownership, speak up, and engage with others confidently. This

---

[18] The 5 Levels Of Team Trust: Mastering Remote Work Dynamics https://www.forbes.com/councils/forbescoachescouncil/2024/07/11/the-5-levels-of-team-trust-mastering-remote-work-dynamics/

is especially important for newly appointed leaders who are still developing their leadership identity or new members of the team.

When people trust themselves, they:

- Contribute ideas without waiting for permission
- Take responsibility for their work and decisions
- Recognize and build on their own growth

As a leader, you can support self-trust by acknowledging not just outcomes but effort and progress. Celebrate learning—not just winning.

Level 2: Interpersonal Trust

Next comes reliability. Do people follow through on commitments? Do they communicate openly about progress or challenges? This level of trust is about consistency—knowing that others will deliver, and that it's safe to depend on each other.

At this level, you'll see behaviors like:

- Timely updates on progress
- Willingness to ask for and offer help
- Dependable execution

You can strengthen this trust by creating space for connection— casual conversations at the start of meetings, regular 1:1s, and time to align beyond just task updates.

Level 3: Competence Trust

Once reliability is established, the next layer is confidence in each other's *expertise*. This is where collaboration deepens. Team members trust that their peers bring value—and aren't afraid to lean on them for input or delegate responsibility.

When competence trust is present:

- People share knowledge openly.
- Constructive feedback flows naturally.
- Team members recognize and rely on each other's strengths.

To build it, host knowledge-sharing sessions, set up mentoring pairs, and publicly recognize the expertise each person brings to the team.

Level 4: Emotional Trust

This is the turning point. Emotional trust means people can be real with each other. They don't just talk about work—they talk about how they work together. They share concerns. They offer feedback that's sometimes hard to hear. And they know it won't be held against them.

At this level:

- People challenge each other with respect.
- Difficult topics are raised early, not avoided.
- Feedback is shared honestly and received constructively.

You can support this by inviting reflection regularly—what's going well, what's getting in the way, and what needs to be said. And when someone speaks up, show them they were right to do so by how you respond.

Level 5: Team Synergy

At the top of the trust pyramid is synergy—the point at which the team acts as a truly cohesive unit. People don't just cooperate; they anticipate one another, challenge one another, and build on one another's ideas. Trust is embedded in every interaction.

When synergy is strong:

- The team solves problems collectively.
- Shared goals are prioritized over individual wins.
- Stakeholder needs are anticipated and integrated.

Your role as a leader at this stage is to *sustain* trust. That means reinforcing the five pillars you've built throughout this book: Clear Purpose, Linking Connections, Integrated Work, Collaborative Decisions, and Knowledge Sharing.

If your team struggles to surface tension or engage in real disagreement, it's likely they're stuck at one of the earlier stages of trust. Focus on building or rebuilding trust at the first layer and see how people become more ready to address issues they used to shy away from.

Conflict itself doesn't destroy trust. But when you're avoiding it, it's a clear signal that it's not safe to speak up.

Use Feedback to Catch Issues Early

Conflict rarely arrives all at once. It tends to build gradually—in the form of small misunderstandings, subtle frustrations, or feedback that was never given. One of the most effective ways to prevent conflict debt from accumulating is to create consistent opportunities for people to speak up— early and often.

As discussed in the previous chapter, feedback doesn't need to be a formal event. In high-functioning teams, it's part of the day-to-day. The more regularly teams reflect on how they're working—together and individually—the easier it becomes to address tension while it's still manageable.

Apart from the feedback practices we shared earlier in the previous chapter, you can use Peer Feedback Pairs.

Once a month, invite team members to pair up for brief feedback exchanges. The goal isn't a full performance review—it's a structured, focused conversation. You can offer two prompts:

- One thing I appreciated about working with you this month was...
- One thing I'd suggest doing differently next time is...

This helps team members build comfort with giving and receiving feedback outside of formal channels. It also reinforces the idea that feedback is everyone's responsibility—not just the manager's.

Rotating partners over time helps strengthen trust across the team and prevents silos from forming.

Run Conflict-Resolving Retrospectives

Retrospectives are often viewed as a way to review project outcomes—what went well, what didn't, and what to adjust next time. But their real potential goes beyond process improvement. When used intentionally, retrospectives can become one of the most effective tools for addressing conflict debt and restoring trust within a team.

Too often, teams reflect on timelines, deliverables, and outcomes, while leaving interpersonal dynamics and underlying tension off the table. That's a missed opportunity. When a team has the structure, facilitation, and trust to reflect on *how* they worked together—not just *what* they did—it becomes possible to address unresolved issues before they become embedded patterns.

A well-run retrospective provides three essential functions:

1. It gives the team space to slow down and examine what they've been avoiding.
2. It creates shared language around moments of friction or misalignment.

3. It helps the team move forward with clarity and renewed accountability.

A Format for Conflict-Focused Retrospectives

When the goal is to surface and resolve interpersonal or team-level tension—not just debrief a project—your format needs to guide the conversation toward honest reflection. Here's a structure that works well for that purpose:

1. **Set the Tone**

Open by naming the purpose: This is a chance to step back and look at not only the work but also the way the team worked together. Make it clear that the goal is learning and improvement, not blame. Reaffirm the expectation of respectful dialogue and mutual curiosity.

2. **Start → Stop → Continue**

Begin with familiar ground. Ask team members to reflect on:

- What should we start doing that could help us work better together?
- What should we stop doing that's getting in the way?
- What should we continue doing that's working?

This gives people a structured, non-threatening entry point into reflection.

3. **Surface Tension**

Once the group is warmed up, shift to more direct prompts:

- What caused friction during this cycle or project?
- Was there anything we didn't say at the time that would've helped?
- What conversations have we been postponing?

Encourage specificity. The aim here is not to relive old arguments, but to name dynamics that might otherwise stay beneath the surface.

4. Understand the Impact

Next, help the team examine the cost of unresolved tension:

- What did it cost us not to address this earlier?
- How did it affect our collaboration, speed, or outcomes?

This reflection shifts the focus from individual behavior to shared responsibility.

5. Build Agreements

Close by aligning on what needs to change. Ask:

- What will we do differently going forward?
- What support or structure will help us stick to these changes?

Write down clear, collective commitments. Assign ownership if needed, and agree on a time to revisit progress.

The Role of the Facilitator

Retrospectives that touch on conflict require thoughtful facilitation. This doesn't always mean bringing in an external coach, but it does require someone who can hold the space neutrally. That person's role is to guide the discussion, ensure everyone's voice is heard, and prevent the conversation from becoming a debate or blame session.

In some cases, it makes sense for the team leader to facilitate. In others—especially where trust is fragile—asking someone else to guide the session may make it easier for people to speak candidly.

The Silence Was the Signal

When Clair took over a business unit at FastGrowingCompany Inc., everything looked fine on paper. Deadlines were technically being met. No major issues were being raised in meetings. Her direct reports were competent and experienced. But something didn't feel right.

Delivery timelines began to slip—just slightly at first. Then more frequently. A few team members left unexpectedly, and exit interviews revealed vague answers about "fit" and "communication." Still, in team meetings, no one raised any red flags. Everyone said they were aligned. Everyone said things were fine.

Clair wasn't convinced.

Rather than push harder for answers in group settings, she created space for honesty in a different way. She introduced a simple anonymous feedback exercise. Team members were asked to answer three questions:

- What do we need to change to be a better team?
- How can we better support each other?
- What's one thing holding us back from working at our best?

The responses were eye-opening. Frustrations that had been lingering for months—some, even years—suddenly surfaced. Team members shared concerns about misaligned priorities, a lack of follow-through on commitments, and a culture of "false agreement" in meetings.

Clair didn't try to resolve everything at once. Instead, she shifted the team into a new rhythm: short, focused retrospectives at the end of each cycle—not just to review work but to reflect on how they worked together. She added in regular "What's Working / What's Not" check-ins and created informal spaces for peer feedback.

Over time, the tone of the team changed. People became more candid. They started naming issues earlier. When there was disagreement, it was handled in the room—not in hallway conversations afterward. Slowly, the group moved from avoiding conflict to using it productively.

Six months later, the team was collaborating more effectively and feeling more engaged. Other teams in the organization began asking to borrow Clair's retrospective format. It had become a model for how to lead through silence and rebuild trust through structure.

Conflict debt doesn't always announce itself. It builds quietly—in the spaces between conversations. A meeting that ends too quickly. A decision no one questions. A team that's polite—but no longer challenging each other.

When teams don't speak up, leaders often assume everything is fine. But the absence of tension isn't a sign of strength—it's a sign to investigate. Because teams that grow together aren't the ones that avoid conflict. They're the ones that know how to engage with it, address it, and learn from it.

This chapter has offered a structure for doing just that. You've explored how to spot early signs of unresolved tension, how to build the trust necessary for difficult conversations, and how to make feedback a regular part of your team's rhythm. You've seen how retrospectives can become tools not just for reflection but for repair. And you've looked at how to move past the illusion of agreement toward something more valuable—shared understanding.

What matters most is consistency. Turn it into leadership practice. One that signals: We talk about what matters—even when it's hard. And we do it not to be right, but to get better.

Teams that learn how to surface tension early and address it constructively are more innovative, more cohesive, and far better positioned to do meaningful work, together.

CHAPTER 15

REFLECT, RESET, REPEAT: MAKING GROWTH A TEAM HABIT

If you asked me what the most powerful way to transform a team is, I'd say reflection. Without hesitation.

Reflection is the moment when a team takes a pause to ask themselves: What's working? What isn't? What do we want to keep doing, stop doing, or change? These are simple questions, but when they're asked consistently—and answered honestly—they create a kind of team intelligence that no tool or training can replicate.

And you probably have done some of it already. But the real power reveals itself only when reflection becomes a cultural habit. It's how teams build shared awareness, course-correct before issues spiral, and reinforce the behaviors they want to see more of. It's the habit that keeps you learning as you go.

Self-sufficient CLICK teams treat reflection as part of how they work, not something they squeeze in when everything else is done. And that's why they get better over time—because they've built a rhythm for learning, together.

If you want to create a resilient, engaged, self-steering team, start here.

Why Teams Avoid Reflection—And What They Miss

Most teams don't reflect regularly—and they have plenty of reasons for it.

"We don't have time."

"We already know what went wrong."

"We're busy fixing things."

These answers might feel valid in the moment, but they cover up the real issue: Reflection hasn't been built into the rhythm of work. It's not protected, and it's not expected. So it gets pushed aside by whatever feels more urgent.

But when teams skip reflection, everything you've done before—discovering team purpose, building a living ecosystem with the team's stakeholders and other teams in the organization, designing work processes and decision-making strategies—all goes in vain. When teams don't make time to pause and talk about what's happening, they start repeating the same avoidable mistakes. Small issues snowball. Wins go unrecognized. And people get tired of putting in effort without ever stepping back to understand what's really driving results—or blocking them.

Here's what gets lost when reflection is missing:

- Recurring issues go unresolved. Instead of fixing the root cause, teams keep patching the symptoms.

- People burn out from repetition. The same problems keep showing up, and solving them starts to feel like a loop.

- What's working doesn't get scaled. Successes stay invisible, and no one knows what to replicate.

- Engagement drops. When people don't have space to speak up or see progress, they disengage. Not out of laziness—out of frustration.

And most importantly—without reflection, your team doesn't know if they are moving in the right direction. And when they don't, they come to you. Again. And again. And again, until you're caught up once more in the cycle of managing your team's operations instead of growing a self-sufficient team that lets you focus on what only you can do best.

Make It Part of the Rhythm

Reflection only works when it becomes part of how your team operates—not a one-off event, not something that depends on who's in the room, and definitely not something that happens only after a crisis.

The key is rhythm. Just like you'd never run a team without regular check-ins or planning sessions, reflection needs its own place in the calendar as a core part of how the team improves.

There's no one-size-fits-all approach. What matters is co-creating a rhythm with your team that fits your workflow, your pace, and your style. Some teams build it into their quarterly strategy sessions. Others hold retrospectives at the end of each sprint, or schedule mini reflections every Friday to check in on collaboration and energy. Many run post-mortems after big launches, and some even start projects with a pre-mortem to name risks before they happen. If you don't recognize those don't worry—we'll describe them later in this chapter.

You don't need hours to do this well. Repetition and conscience always win. Even 30 minutes—done regularly, with the right structure—can reshape how your team thinks, talks, and acts.

Here's what that could look like:

- A short async check-in at the end of each week: *What's one thing we learned? What's one thing we'd change?*
- A 45-minute reflection after each project or major milestone.
- A monthly or quarterly team session focused on how you're working together, not just what you're delivering.

The rhythm you choose should fit your team's context. What matters most is that it exists. Because without rhythm, reflection becomes a good intention. With rhythm, it becomes a habit.

How do you create the right rhythm? There is only one way to know— try it and see what works best for your team.

Different Types of Reflection—and When to Use Them

Not all reflection looks the same. Depending on where your team is in the cycle—starting a project, wrapping one up, regrouping after a tough quarter, or trying to work better together—you'll need different approaches.

So let's look at different types of reflection sessions you can have with your team.

1. Pre-Mortem: Spot Problems Before They Happen

Use this when: You're kicking off a new project, initiative, or decision.

This is your chance to pause before the work begins and ask: *What could go wrong?*

You ask the team to imagine it's six months from now, and the project has failed. Then you ask: What happened? What did we overlook? What assumptions didn't hold? What risks did we ignore?

It's a safe way to surface concerns early—before anyone's too invested or committed. And it helps the team align on risk, pressure points, and what to watch for—together.

2. Post-Mortem: Learn from What Just Happened

Use this when: You've finished a project, launch, or major decision.

I've heard people saying—we don't need post-mortem, the launch was successful. But this session isn't just about what went wrong—it's about what worked, what you'd repeat, and what you'd change next time.

It's important to keep the tone constructive. Focus on the future, like we did with the Future-Focused Feedback. Invite multiple perspectives, use real data where you can, and discuss patterns—not personalities.

A strong post-mortem helps teams evolve faster by pulling insights forward into the next cycle.

3. Retrospective: Check In on Team Dynamics

Use this when: You want to step back from tasks and look at how the team is functioning.

Retrospectives are typically done on a regular basis—monthly, bi-weekly, or quarterly—and they focus on how the team is working together.

They're great for surfacing hidden friction, naming what's helping or hurting the flow of work, and updating team agreements if needed.

Try prompts like:

- What should we start, stop, and continue?
- What made this period easier—or harder—than it needed to be?
- How did we handle disagreement or feedback?

This kind of reflection helps teams co-create the working processes and master the integrated work pillar of the CLICK framework.

4. Collaboration and Relationship Check-ins: Reflect on How You're Working Together

Use this when: Trust, communication, or alignment needs attention.

Sometimes, the work is fine—but the way people are working together isn't.

Use this format to check in on relationships: Are we hearing each other? Are we showing up for one another? Are we aligned on what matters? These are especially important in hybrid or distributed teams, or after team changes.

They can be standalone sessions—or part of a larger reflection.

Even a short conversation about *how* you're collaborating can reset the tone and create space for deeper trust.

5. Stakeholder Reflections: Look Beyond the Team

Use this when: You want to reflect on how your work is landing with others.

Sometimes the most valuable feedback isn't from inside the team. It's from the people you serve—clients, internal partners, senior leaders.

These sessions help the team look outward and reflect on questions like:

- Are we delivering what others need?
- What feedback have we been hearing—but not acting on?
- How are we impacting others' ability to do their jobs?

These reflections keep the team grounded in real impact—not just internal process.

Each of these formats serves a different purpose. When used together, they create a full picture—not just of what your team is doing but how it's growing.

How to Run an Effective Reflection Session

The main element of a good reflection session is a genuine intention to learn and the meeting structure you decide upon. For some high-stakes sessions, you might want to invite a professional facilitator, but it's not necessary for the majority of your team sessions. What's important is that you have a clear goal, make space for different voices, and ensure the insights lead to action.

Whether you're doing this in-person, remotely, or asynchronously, the same principles apply.

Before the Session

Set the intention.

What do you want to learn or shift? Are you focusing on a project, a process, or the team dynamic? Make that clear up front so people know what lens to bring.

Choose a structure.

Let the team know what format you'll be using—whether it's a Start/Stop/Continue, a post-mortem, or a check-in on collaboration.

Prep the space.

If the session is live, prepare prompts and a way to capture ideas (Miro board, shared doc, whiteboard).

If it's async, send out a reflection board or doc in advance so people can add input at their own pace.

Optional—but helpful: Collect anonymous input ahead of time. This can surface concerns that people might hesitate to share out loud.

During the Session

Start with facts.

Open with data, not opinions. This keeps the conversation grounded. For example: "Here's what we set out to do. Here's what happened. Here's what we delivered."

Create space for all voices.

Some people will speak easily. Others won't. Use prompts or round-robin questions to make sure everyone contributes. Or use silent writing time before discussion to give people space to think.

Use simple, structured prompts.

Don't ask vague questions like "So… how did that go?" Instead, try:

- What helped us succeed?
- Where did we get stuck?
- What would we try differently next time?

Capture key takeaways in real time.

Use a visible space where people can see their feedback being recorded. It builds trust and accountability.

After the Session

Summarize what you heard.

Send out a short summary: what the team reflected on, what's changing, what's staying the same. This shows people that their input mattered.

Follow through.

If someone said, "We need to meet earlier in the week to align," don't wait for the next retro to revisit it. Put a change in motion.

Circle back.

In the next session, revisit what was agreed last time. Ask: Did we actually do it? What impact did it have?

A Few Common Pitfalls to Avoid

- **Turning the session into a complaint spiral.** Reflection isn't venting. Guide the team back to learning: *What's in our control? What could we try differently next time?*

- **Letting one person dominate.** Use prompts, timers, or round-robin check-ins to keep the space balanced.

- **Treating it like a performance review.** This isn't about judging people—it's about understanding what the team needs to work better together.

- **Skipping follow-up.** If nothing changes after the session, people stop showing up honestly. Trust is built by action.

- **Doing it all yourself.** It's fine to lead these at first, but start pulling in co-facilitators. Let project leads run reflections for their projects.

For reflection sessions to work, many things need to happen beforehand—people need to feel safe to share concerns, the team manager needs the skills to share facts, not opinions, and the team needs a desire to learn and grow together. But even when you don't have it all yet, reflections contribute to everything else you are doing to build a real CLICK team.

Reflection sessions don't need to be perfect. They need to be intentional, inclusive, and followed by movement. That's how you shift a team from reacting to learning.

How Reflection Changed My Team

When I stepped into the Chief People Officer role in a cloud computing company, I inherited a team that had been through too many transitions. In just over a year, they'd seen two or three different leaders cycle through the position. Trust was low, morale was worse, and the team was running on fumes—both in terms of people and energy.

Some had already disengaged quietly. Others were openly frustrated. A few new hires were just trying to find their footing in the middle of the chaos. We weren't just understaffed—we were unanchored.

We couldn't fix everything overnight. But we could start talking. So that's what we did.

We created a steady rhythm of strategy and reflection sessions— every quarter, without fail. These weren't long-winded meetings filled with slides and updates. They were intentional pauses where we asked real questions:

- What did we actually accomplish?
- What challenges did we face?
- What's getting in our way?
- Are we being the team we want to be?

Each session helped us look forward, but it also gave us a moment to look inward. And one of the most powerful tools we introduced was something incredibly simple: appreciation.

We created a shared board—just a Miro space, nothing fancy. Every person had their own section. During the session, we each took time to write messages of gratitude and recognition for our colleagues. The only rule was: be specific. Not "great job"—but "I appreciated the way you stepped in to lead that project while juggling so many other priorities. You kept us moving."

Some messages were anonymous. Others were signed. But the impact was visible.

At first, people were hesitant. A little awkward. But round after round, quarter after quarter, the tone started to shift. People looked forward to those sessions. They wanted to see what their teammates had noticed.

They wanted to express what they hadn't had time—or courage—to say out loud before.

And what started with appreciation expanded into action. We talked about how we were collaborating, how we were showing up for each other, and how we could get better. We reflected not just on our output but on our identity as a team.

Eventually, something changed. The surveys showed it first—we became the most engaged team in the organization. But more than that, the CEO called us out directly: "This is one of the best teams in terms of true collaboration. You're showing others what good looks like."

These moments of reflection gave us space to heal, space to grow, and to actually become the kind of team we wanted to be.

Of course, there was a lot of other work happening alongside those quarterly reflections—restructuring, hiring, resetting expectations. But the rhythm of reflection created the structure and support the team needed to navigate those challenges together.

That's the power of reflection. When it becomes part of the culture, everything else can shift around it.

Reflection is one of the most underused tools in team leadership—and one of the most powerful.

In this chapter, you've seen how consistent reflection helps teams not only learn from their work but shape how they work together. You've explored the five different types of reflection—from pre-mortems and post-mortems to team dynamics and stakeholder check-ins. You've seen how small, structured conversations can turn scattered feedback into shared learning—and how regular rhythm builds trust, clarity, and alignment over time.

You've also seen that reflection isn't just a meeting format. It's a culture-building habit. A way for your team to pause, learn, and adjust—without waiting for things to break.

And you've read what happened when one team made reflection part of their DNA. It didn't require big change management plans. Just commitment, consistency, and a willingness to learn out loud.

When reflection becomes part of how a team operates, everything else gets easier. Problems are caught earlier. Wins are repeated more often. People feel heard, valued, and ready to lead alongside you—not just follow behind.

So don't wait for the perfect moment. Choose a format. Invite your team in. And start building the habit that changes everything.

EPILOGUE

ONE STEP AT A TIME

By now, you've walked through the five pillars of the CLICK framework—Clear Purpose, Linking Connections, Integrated Work, Collaborative Decisions, and Knowledge Sharing. Together, they form the foundation for building teams that are both high-performing at the moment, and self-sustaining over time.

Each pillar matters. Each one strengthens the others. But if you feel like there's a lot to take in, you're right. That's because building a team that can truly click isn't a weekend project—it's an ongoing practice.

This book isn't meant to be a checklist you sprint through and file away. Think of it instead as a toolkit. A field guide. Something you can return to again and again as you and your team grow. The real transformation happens not through perfect execution, but through real-world experimentation—trying, adjusting, learning, and trying again.

Pick one idea that resonated with you. Maybe it's shaping a purpose statement your team can actually connect with. Or setting clearer norms around decision-making. Or finally running meetings that invite—and actually hear—every voice.

Start there.

Talk with your team. Ask them what's working, what's frustrating, and where they're hungry to do better. Change sticks when it's co-created, not imposed. You don't need all the answers upfront. You just need to begin the conversation—and be willing to listen.

By putting these small shifts into motion, you're doing more than just improving performance. You're building a team that knows how to think together, challenge one another, and move forward—without waiting for top-down direction. That kind of trust and independence doesn't happen overnight. It's built conversation by conversation, experiment by experiment.

When you're ready to go even further—whether it's mapping your team's maturity, strengthening your work with stakeholders, or navigating tougher dynamics—you'll find more tools waiting for you. On my website, you'll find downloadable materials: checklists, templates, team exercises, even Miro boards you can customize. Use what fits your current needs, and come back for more when you're ready.

Building a CLICK team isn't about perfection. It's about commitment.

And if you get stuck, know this: Help is just a click away. Reach out through my website—I'd love to hear how your journey is going.

We've outgrown the era of heroic leadership. It's time to build something better: empowered, self-sufficient teams that can adapt, thrive, and lead themselves into the future.

ACKNOWLEDGMENTS

Writing this book was never something I did alone. Every step of the way, it was shaped by conversations, advice, encouragement—and a lot of patience—from people who believed in the work before it fully came together.

I'm deeply grateful to Erik Seversen, whose steady guidance helped me navigate the publishing process when it felt overwhelming. Your encouragement gave me the momentum to keep moving forward, one piece at a time.

A heartfelt thank you to Beverly West for jumping in early, offering sharp insights, and helping to turn a jumble of ideas into something real. You helped this book find its shape and its voice.

To Jesan Sorrells, John Knotts, Gary Burke, and Paz Itzhaki Weinberger—thank you for sharing your stories as authors. Your openness gave me not just ideas, but the permission to begin, and the reminder that momentum matters more than perfection.

I'm also grateful to Veiko Valkiainen, Sebastian Gerhardt, and Dr. David Leitner for the ideas and perspectives you shared so generously. Some of them live in the pages of this book; others continue to grow in the conversations we're having beyond it, including on my YouTube channel.

To the friends and family who stood by me—thank you. Your encouragement, your late-night texts, your willingness to listen to me talk through a half-formed idea (for the fifth time)—all of it made this possible.

To the early readers who challenged assumptions, flagged confusing sections, and asked the kinds of sharp, thoughtful questions that helped me clarify my thinking—thank you. Many of the tools and exercises in this book were born as direct responses to those conversations. You helped me see what leaders truly needed, not just what I thought they needed. That made this book better, more relevant, and more grounded in the real-world challenges teams face.

This book is better because of you—and because of the small, important ways you reminded me to trust the work and keep going.

ABOUT THE AUTHOR

Daria Rudnik is a team architect and executive leadership coach with over 15 years of global executive experience, including roles at Deloitte and as a former chief people officer in tech and telecom. Having worked across six continents, she has guided organizations through major challenges such as financial crises, wars, and the COVID-19 pandemic. Daria is the founder of Aidra.AI, an AI coach for leaders in tech. She helps leaders break free from overwork by building self-sufficient teams and stay ahead in a rapidly evolving landscape by leveraging AI for learning and development.

Go to my website to download tool and resources that will help you build self-sufficient teams.

Email: me@dariarudnik.com

Website https://dariarudnik.com/

LinkedIn https://www.linkedin.com/in/dariarudnik/

YouTube https://www.youtube.com/@dariarudnikcoaching

DID YOU ENJOY THIS BOOK?

If you enjoyed reading this book, you can help by suggesting it to someone else you think might like it, and please leave a positive review wherever you purchased it. This does a lot in helping others find the book. We thank you in advance for taking a few moments to do this.

THANK YOU

DISCOVER MORE BY DARIA RUDNIK

15/30 Planner: Your Evergreen Weekly, Monthly, Quarterly, and Yearly Reflection Journal

Achieve massive progress with just 15 minutes a week and 30 minutes a quarter!

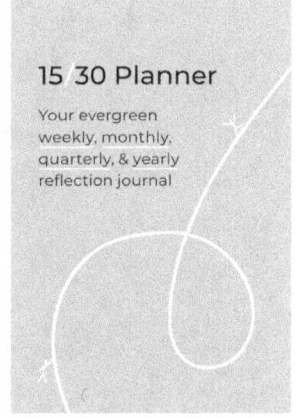

The *15/30 Planner* is built for professionals and leaders who want to stay focused, aligned, and productive without adding more stress to their schedule. With simple weekly reflections, quarterly resets, and yearly visioning — all built around actionable, flexible goals — this evergreen planner helps you stay organized and energized throughout the year.

The AI Revolution: Thriving Within Civilization's Next Big Disruption

The AI Revolution is here. Are you ready?

This book brings together insights from 34 global leaders across tech, government, healthcare, education, and beyond to explore how AI is reshaping our world—what's happening, what's next, and how to thrive in it.

In her chapter, Daria Rudnik focuses on the human side of transformation—highlighting the critical skills teams need to succeed in the AI era, from adaptive thinking to human-AI collaboration.

INDEX

A

accountability, 7-9, 11, 14, 111, 187, 191, 198, 210
action bias, 61-62
action plan, 17, 67, 123, 183
aligning expectations, 107
anonymous:

feedback rounds, 182
notes, 182

asynchronous, 115-117, 126, 132, 134, 136

check-ins, 132
comprehensive, 117, 134
concise, 116, 134

autonomy, 9, 16-17, 27, 100, 137, 142, 151

B

beneficiaries, 73
best follower, 92
best team player, 92
brainstorming solutions, 156

C

Clarity, Role of, 103
clear purpose, 3, 5-6, 12, 97, 102, 122, 196, 215
CLICK framework 3, 97, 207, 215

clear purpose, 3, 196, 215
collaborative decisions, 3, 196, 215
integrated work, 3, 196, 215
knowledge sharing, 3, 196, 215
linking connections 3, 196, 215

CLICK Team Criteria Checklist, 10
client relationship, 112
collaboration, 7-9, 12, 14, 16-17, 26-27, 175-176, 178, 199, 205, 207, 209, 213
collaborative discussion, 108
communication:

matrix, 114-118
plan, 77
types of, 132-133

competence, 142, 149, 194-195,

comprehensive, 73, 115-117, 134
concise, 24, 29, 115, 116, 133, 134, 180
conflict-focused retrospectives, 198
conflict-resolving retrospectives, 197
consensus, 48, 156-157, 162, 189-190

> building, 156
> silent, 190

creativity, 31, 34-36, 42-43, 61, 64, 94, 100, 140
cross-team collaboration, 88
curiosity, 43, 198
customer escalations, 152
cybersecurity:

> group, 79, 83
> team, 78, 81, 83

D

danger zone, 77-78
Deci, Edward, 142
Decision Delegation Grid, 151, 153, 160
decision making:

> in an office, 132
> remotely, 132

decision ownership, 147, 152
decisions:

> high-risk, 152
> high-stakes, 158
> low-risk, 152
> team-wide, 157

digital collaboration tools, 88

disrespectful communication, 48
Drucker, Peter F., 137
dysfunctional dynamics, 2

E

ecosystem, 56, 58, 71, 79, 83-85, 87, 204
effective reflection session, 208
Eisenhower Matrix, 164-165, 168-169
emotional leakage, 190
end users, 78
escalation, 111, 152-154, 161
essential meeting roles, 124
execution, 50-51, 61-62, 88, 118, 121, 127, 140, 151, 168, 194, 215
expectations, 9, 17-18, 23, 30, 99-110, 112, 121, 123, 213
expected outcomes, 103, 106, 123, 127
expected outcomes, 103, 106
external partners, 58, 65, 72, 78,

F

Facilitation of Intrinsic Motivation, 142
facilitator, role of the, 199
Fear-to-Action Flow, 143, 146
feedback requests, types of, 179

> event-based feedback, 180
> future-focused feedback, 180-181
> skill-specific feedback, 179

followership, 91-95
four decision zones, 150

escalated/executive, 151
IC-owned, 151
leader-owned, 150
team-shared, 150

Frankl, Viktor, 5

G

Game Changer Brainstorm
  Session, 120
GC Index, 119
Gerhardt, Sebastian, 147, 217
group discussion, 46, 48, 68
guessing, 99

H

hesitation, 138, 143-144, 151, 158,
  203
high collaboration, 68
high expert knowledge, 153
hybrid teams, 129-131, 136

I

ideation, 61-62
individual meetings, 67-69
individual reflection, 107
individual team members, 3, 39
Influencers, 72
information sharing, 132 134

  in an office, 132
  remotely, 132

information-sharing culture, 49
Inspirational Team Statement, 28
Integrated Work 3, 97-98, 196,
  215, 207

interdependence, 10, 12-14, 18-
  19, 58, 64
internal partners, 56, 71-72, 186,
  208
International Test Commission
  (ITC), 119

J

Jill's fate, 103
Jill's story, 101-104

K

key performance indicators
  (KPIs), 19, 36, 151
key responsibilities, 103

L

lack of ownership, 191
leadership training, 3
Learning & Development (L&D),
  133
learning goals, 34-36
legal exposure, 152
Leitner, David, 91, 217
Living Job Description, 104
long-term shared purpose, 10
low expert knowledge, 153
low feedback activity, 191
low-influence supporters, 78
low-pressure social spaces, 136

M

Mann, Thomas, 97
marketing team brainstorming,
  120
meeting norms, 122-123, 125

micro-collaboration, 60, 136
micro-groups, 63, 64
misalignment, 3, 45, 88, 108, 130, 170, 197
mismatched expectations, 102, 105
mistrust, 2, 14, 23
misunderstandings, 8, 40, 88, 98, 105, 109, 196
Multi-Criteria Decision Analysis (MCDA), 157, 162
multiple channels, 130-132

N

nail roles, 99
Nominal Group Technique (NGT), 155, 162

O

online sessions, 106
open communication, 14, 17, 104, 121, 191
organizational alignment, 22
organization's broader mission, 13, 28
overwhelmed managers, 2
ownership, 10, 52, 54, 58-59, 159-160, 162, 191, 193, 199

P

peer-to-peer interaction, 67
performance goals, 7, 34-36
in-person sessions, 106
pitfalls, 42, 211
planning, 1, 61-62, 82, 109, 118-121, 125, 135, 144, 172, 205

poor communication, 2
prioritization, 163, 168-170, 172
prioritizing values, 47, 48

aspirational values, 47
core values, 47-48
important values, 47
in-person, 45-47
remote, 45-48

R

red lines, 47-49
refinement, 46, 119
reflection, importance of, 211, 213
reflection sessions, types of, 206

collaboration and relationship check-ins, 207
post-mortem, 205-207, 209
pre-mortem, 205-206
retrospective, 205-207
stakeholder reflections, 208

relatedness, 142-143
relationship-building:

In an office, 133
remotely, 133

remote communication, 131
reputational impact, 152
responsibilities, 11-13, 69, 72, 87-88, 97, 99-112, 121
results, 8-9, 11
retail leader, 125
role's purpose, 103
Ryan, Richard, 142

S

scoring, 17, 67, 158
Self-Determination Theory, 142
self-sufficiency, 68, 138
self-sufficient team, 3, 10, 14-15, 18-19, 69, 175, 181, 183, 189, 205, 216
session:

> after, 210-211
> before, 107, 109
> during, 209, 212

shadow zone, 99-104, 110-111
Shadow Zone, 111
shared purpose, 9-10, 12-15, 18-19, 24, 33, 54, 143
SMART goals, 31-32, 34

> achievable, 31-32
> measurable, 31,-36
> relevant, 31-32
> specific, 31-32
> time-bound, 31-32

Stakeholder Engagement Questionnaire, 81
stakeholder inclusion, 74
stakeholders, connections between, 77
strategic goals, 23, 28, 81-82, 164, 171-172
Strategist Visioning Workshop, 120
support zone, 78
synchronous, 115-116, 118, 133-134

> comprehensive, 116, 134
> concise, 116, 133

T

tactical goals, 23
talent acquisition, 84, 86-87
tasks, 8, 10, 12, 21-23, 25, 110-112, 121, 125, 163-172, 192, 207
Team Alignment Map, 87-88, 90, 95
Team Clarity Compass, 105, 107, 109-112

> exercise, 105-106
> works, 105
> workshop, 107-108

team constitution, 39, 41-42
team leaders, 14, 40, 95
Team Maturity Questionnaire, 14-15, 19
team member-owned, 153
Team Purpose Statement, 6, 22, 24, 26-29, 31, 37, 39
team trust, levels of, 193

> competence trust, 194-195
> emotional trust, 195
> interpersonal trust, 194
> self-trust, 193-194
> team synergy, 195

team's core function, 27
teams struggling, 3
template sections, 106
top priorities, 104, 163
transparency, 47, 49-50, 105
trust, 12-14, 16, 48-49

U

unanimous enthusiasm, 157
unclear role definition, 102

V

value exploration, 46
virtual collaboration, 131

> evaluation apprehension, 131
> groupthink, 131, 158
> production blocking, 131
> social loafing, 131

virtual meeting, 88, 129, 131
visual representation, 49, 78

W

working group, 8, 14-15, 17
WOW moments, 52, 53

www.ingramcontent.com/pod-product-compliance
Lightning Source LLC
Chambersburg PA
CBHW061146120626
46546CB00005B/1953